Walt Disney's Lady and the Tramp

TONYS
RESTAURANT

TOKYOPOP®

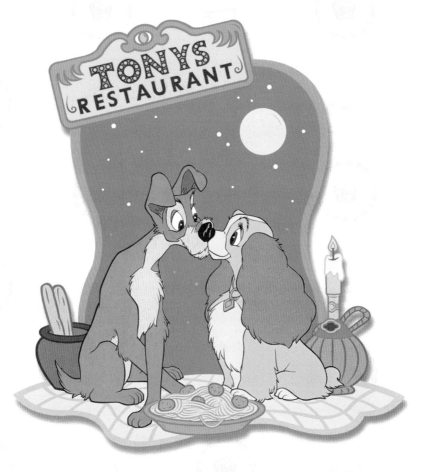

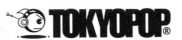

Hamburg • London • Los Angeles • Tokyo

Editor - Erin Stein
Contributing Editor - Kent Hayward
Graphic Designer and Letterer - Monalisa J. de Asis
Cover Designer and Graphic Artist - Anna Kernbaum

Digital Imaging Manager - Chris Buford
Production Managers - Jennifer Miller and Mutsumi Miyazaki
Senior Designer - Anna Kernbaum
Senior Editor - Elizabeth Hurchalla
Managing Editor - Lindsey Johnston
VP of Production - Ron Klamert
Publisher & Editor in Chief - Mike Kiley
President & C.O.O. - John Parker
C.E.O. - Stuart Levy

E-mail: info@TOKYOPOP.com
Come visit us online at www.TOKYOPOP.com

A **TOKYOPOP** Cine-Manga® Book
TOKYOPOP Inc.
5900 Wilshire Blvd., Suite 2000
Los Angeles, CA 90036

Lady and the Tramp

ISBN: 1-59816-443-0

First TOKYOPOP® printing: February 2006

10 9 8 7 6 5 4 3 2 1

Printed in the USA

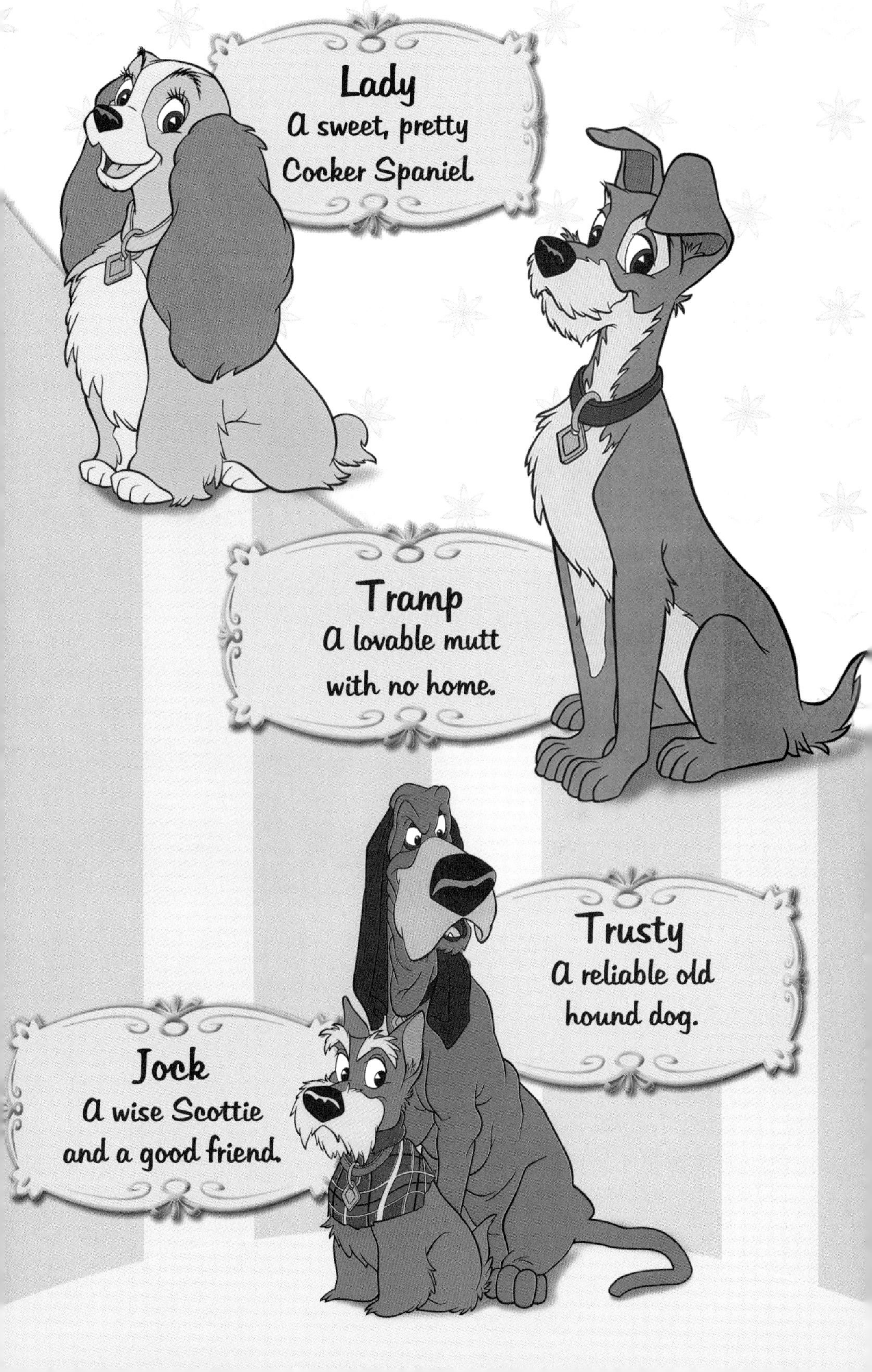
Lady
A sweet, pretty
Cocker Spaniel.
Tramp
A lovable mutt
with no home.
Trusty
A reliable old
hound dog.
Jock
A wise Scottie
and a good friend.

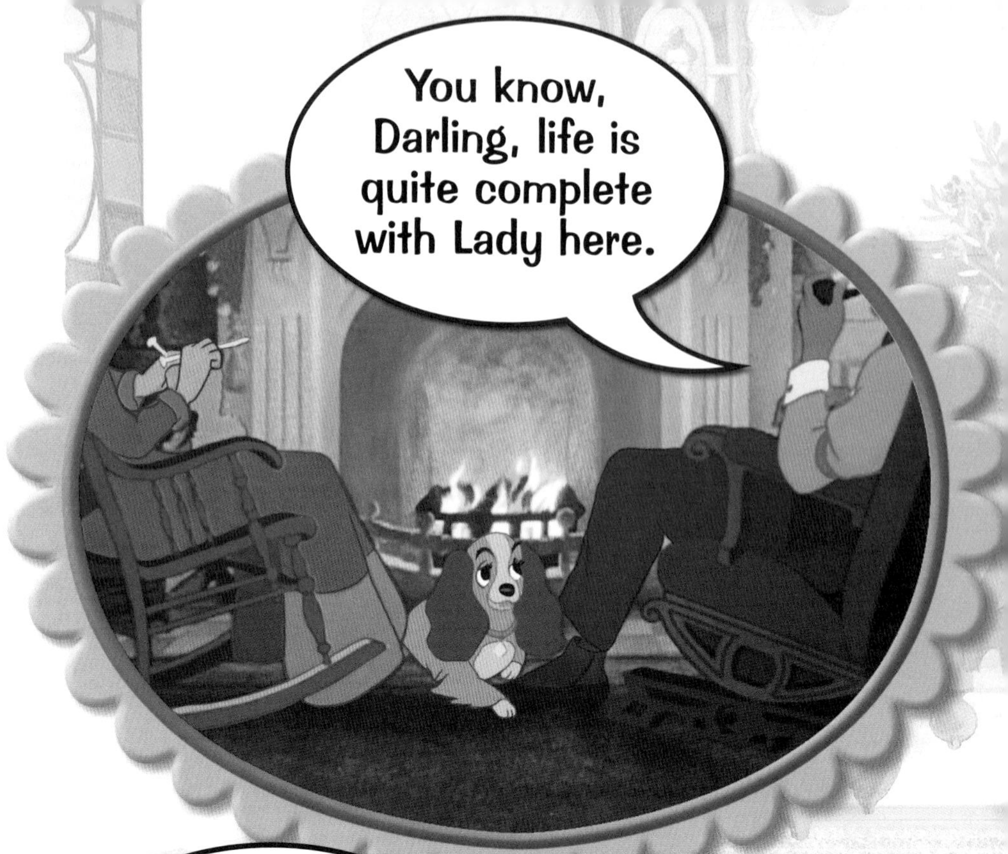
You know, Darling, life is quite complete with Lady here.

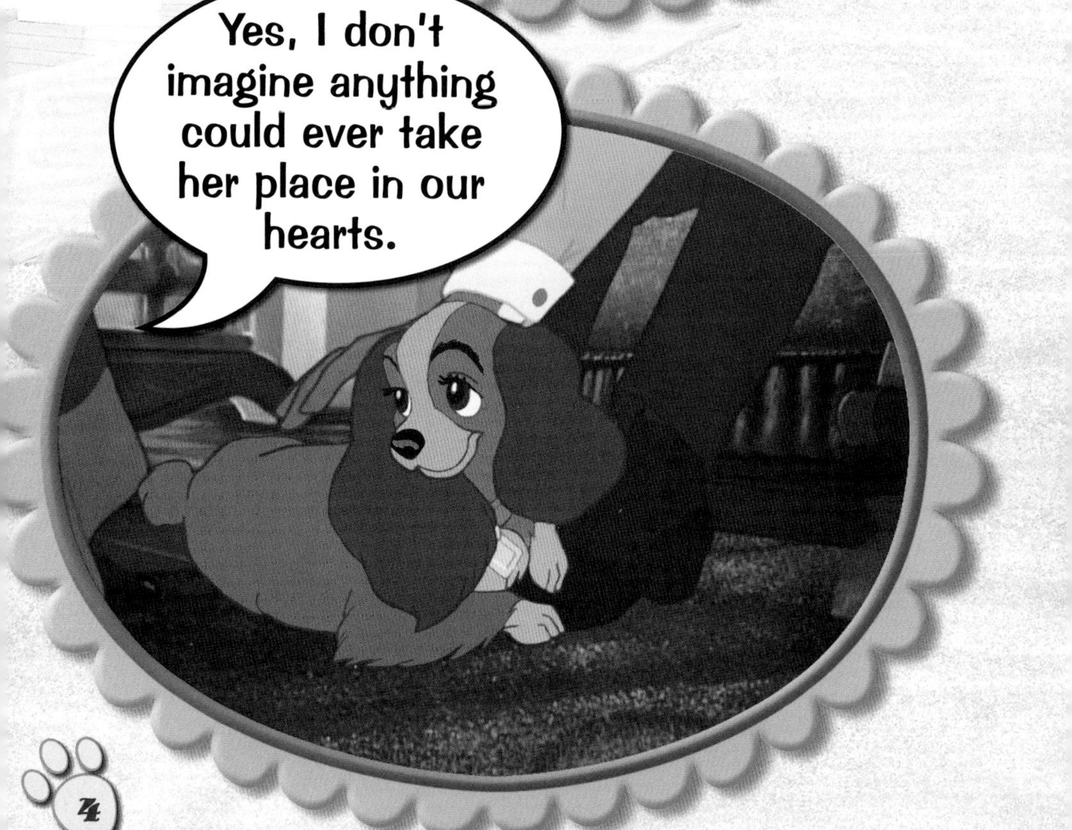
Yes, I don't imagine anything could ever take her place in our hearts.

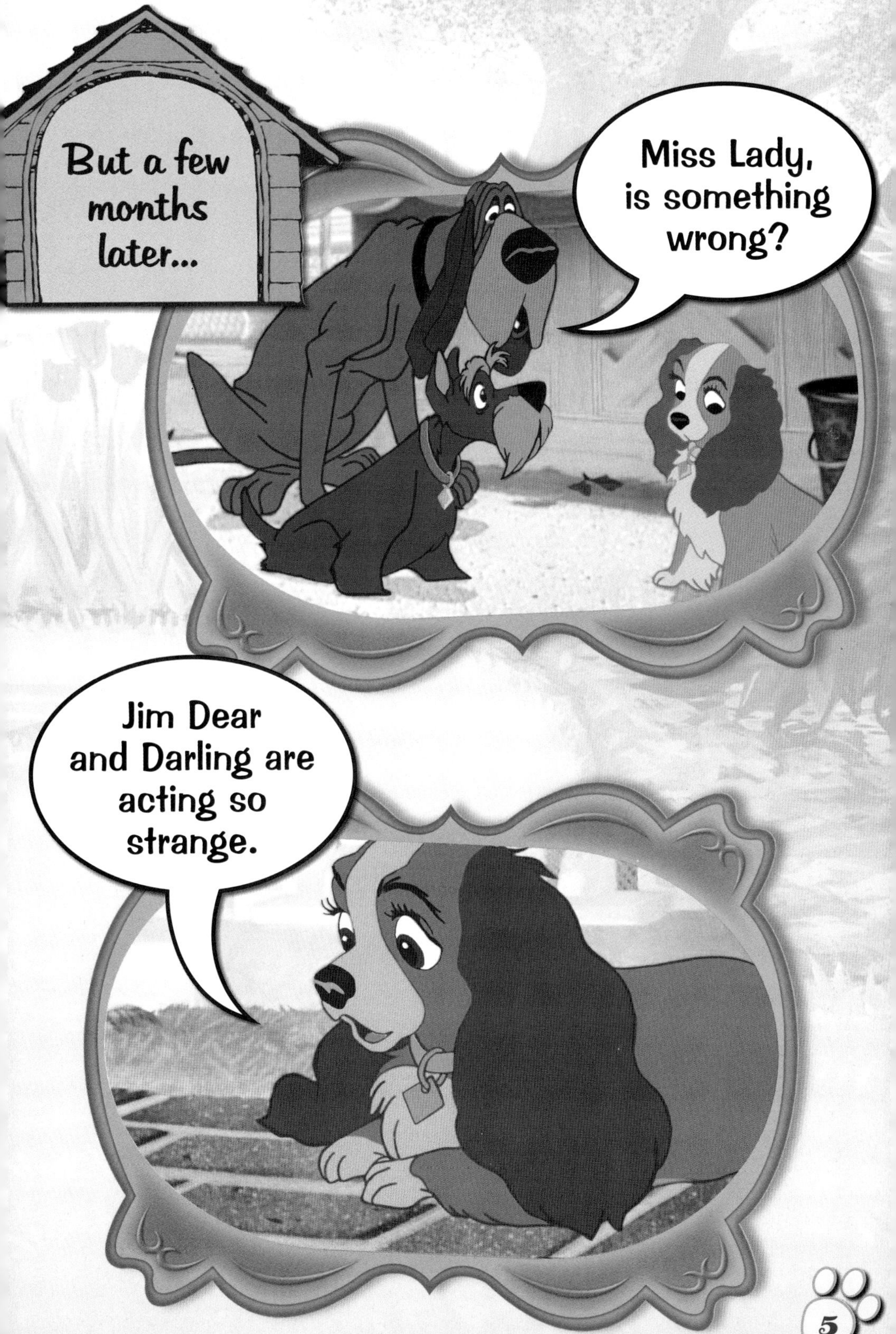
But a few months later...
Miss Lady, is something wrong?
Jim Dear and Darling are acting so strange.

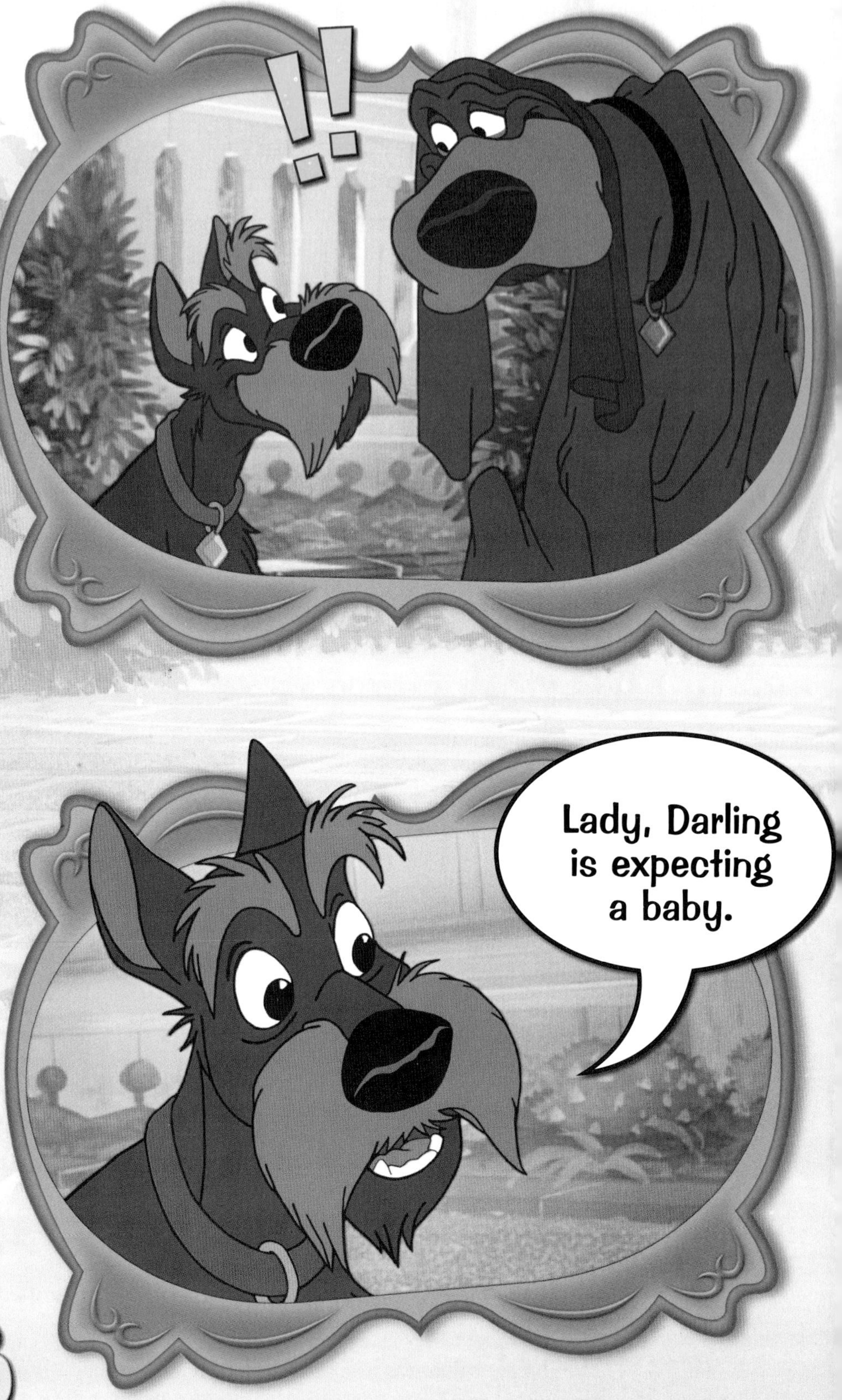
!!
Lady, Darling is expecting a baby.

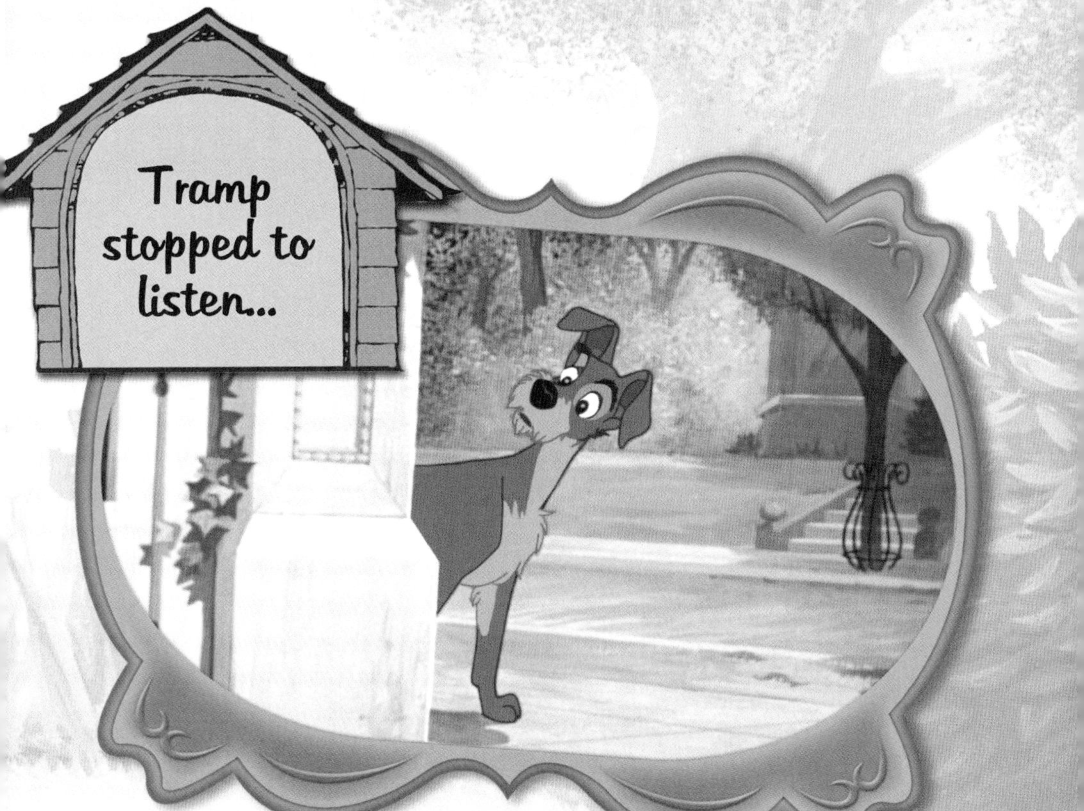
Tramp stopped to listen...

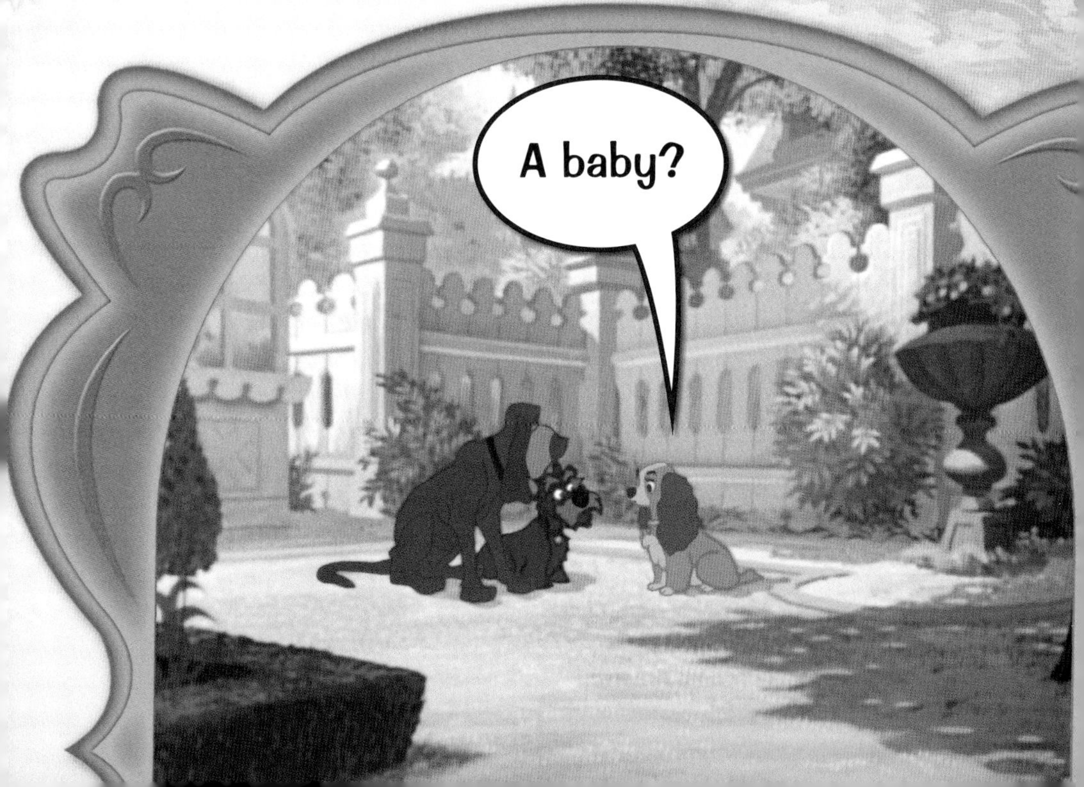
A baby?

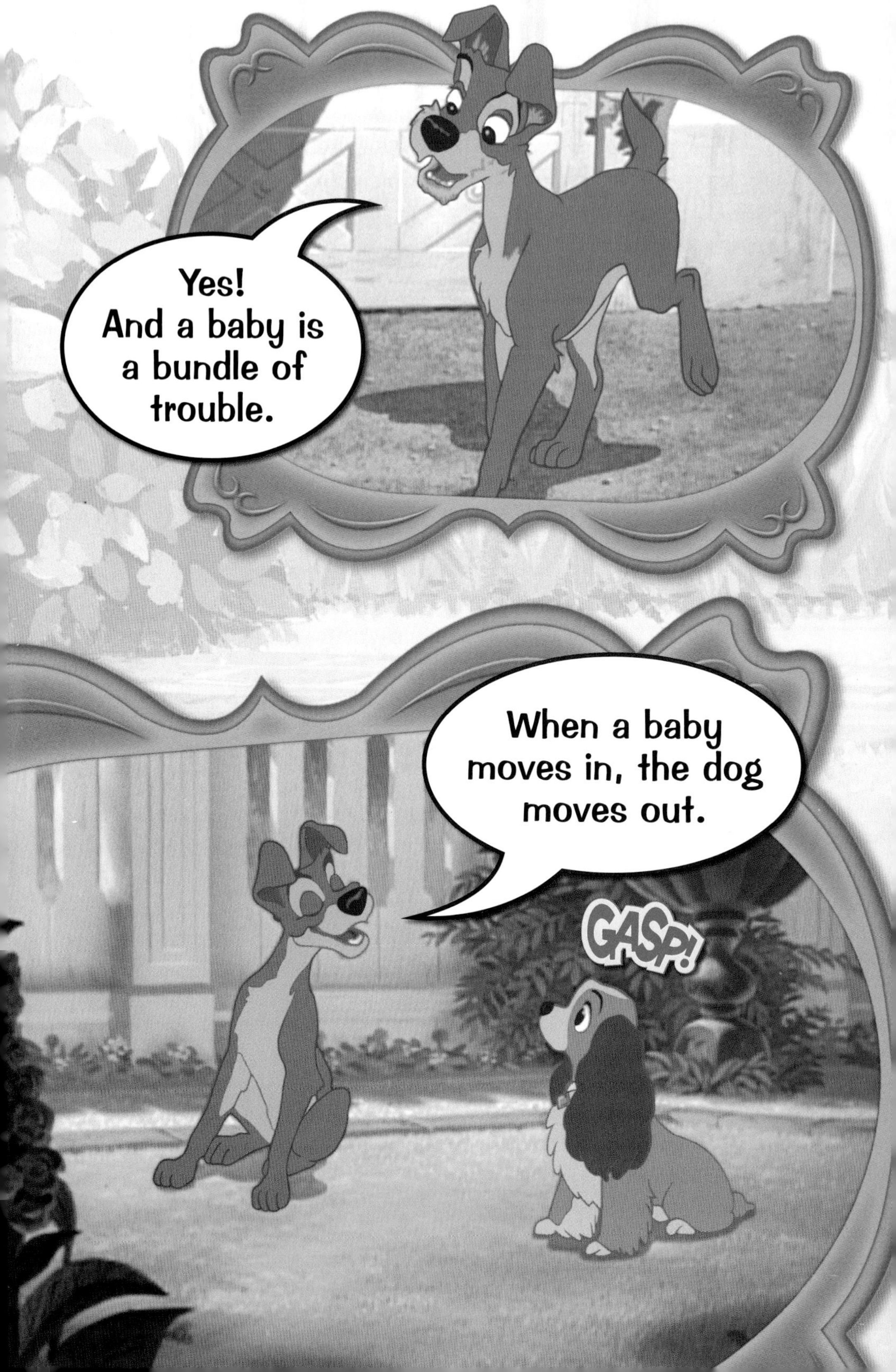
Yes! And a baby is a bundle of trouble.
When a baby moves in, the dog moves out.
GASP!

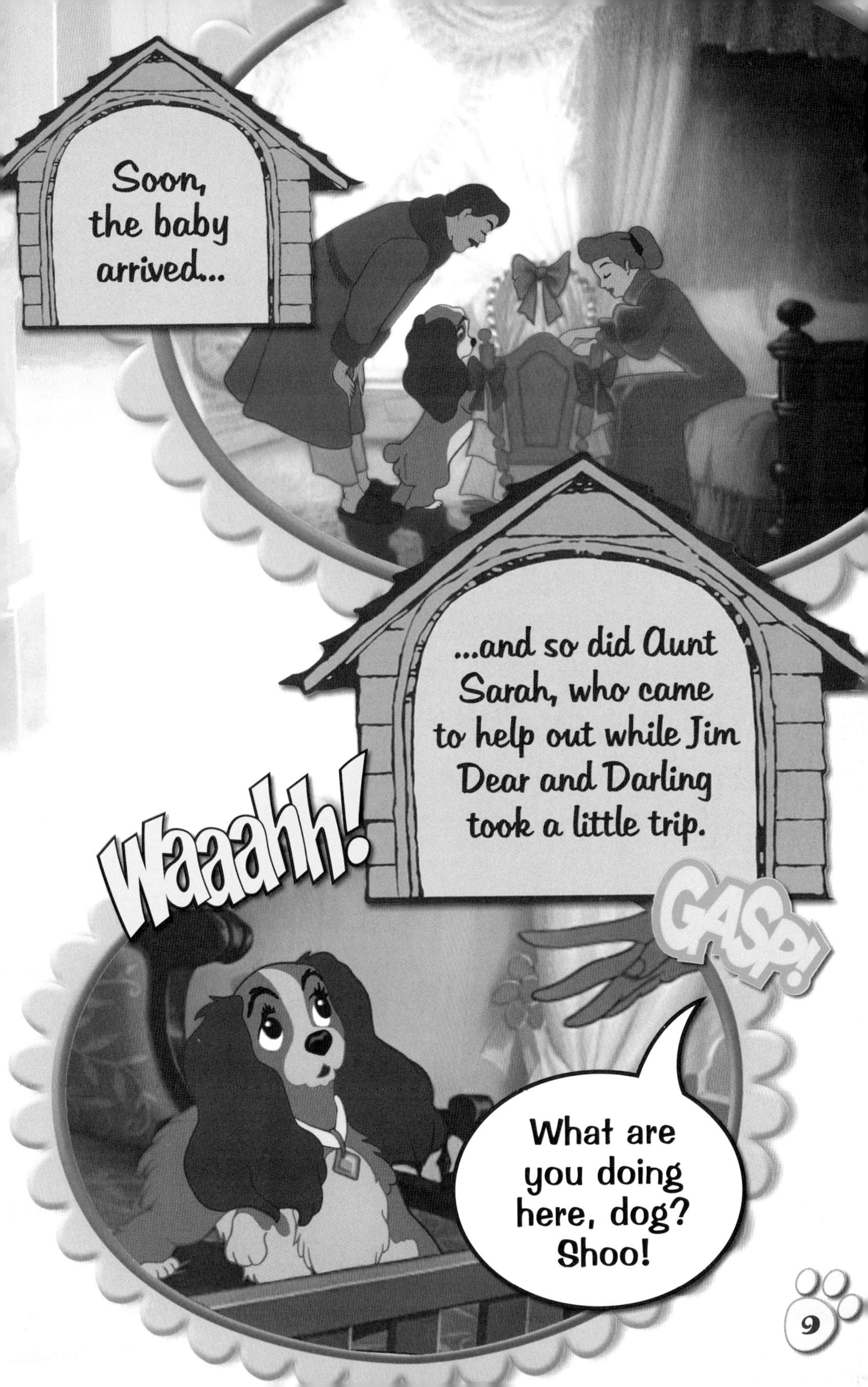
Soon, the baby arrived...
...and so did Aunt Sarah, who came to help out while Jim Dear and Darling took a little trip.
Waaahh!
GASP!
What are you doing here, dog? Shoo!

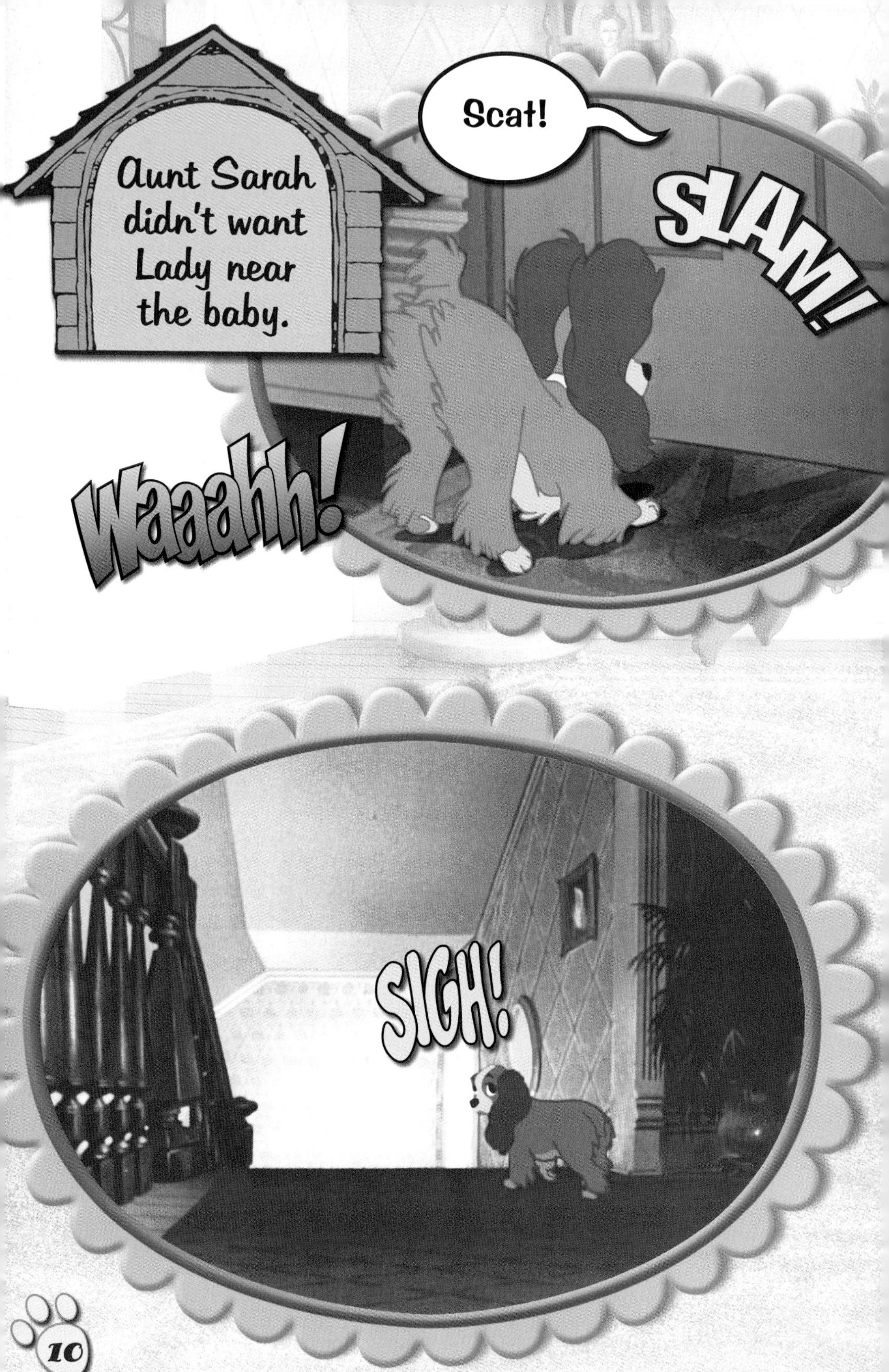
Aunt Sarah didn't want Lady near the baby.
Scat!
SLAM!
Waaahh!
SIGH!

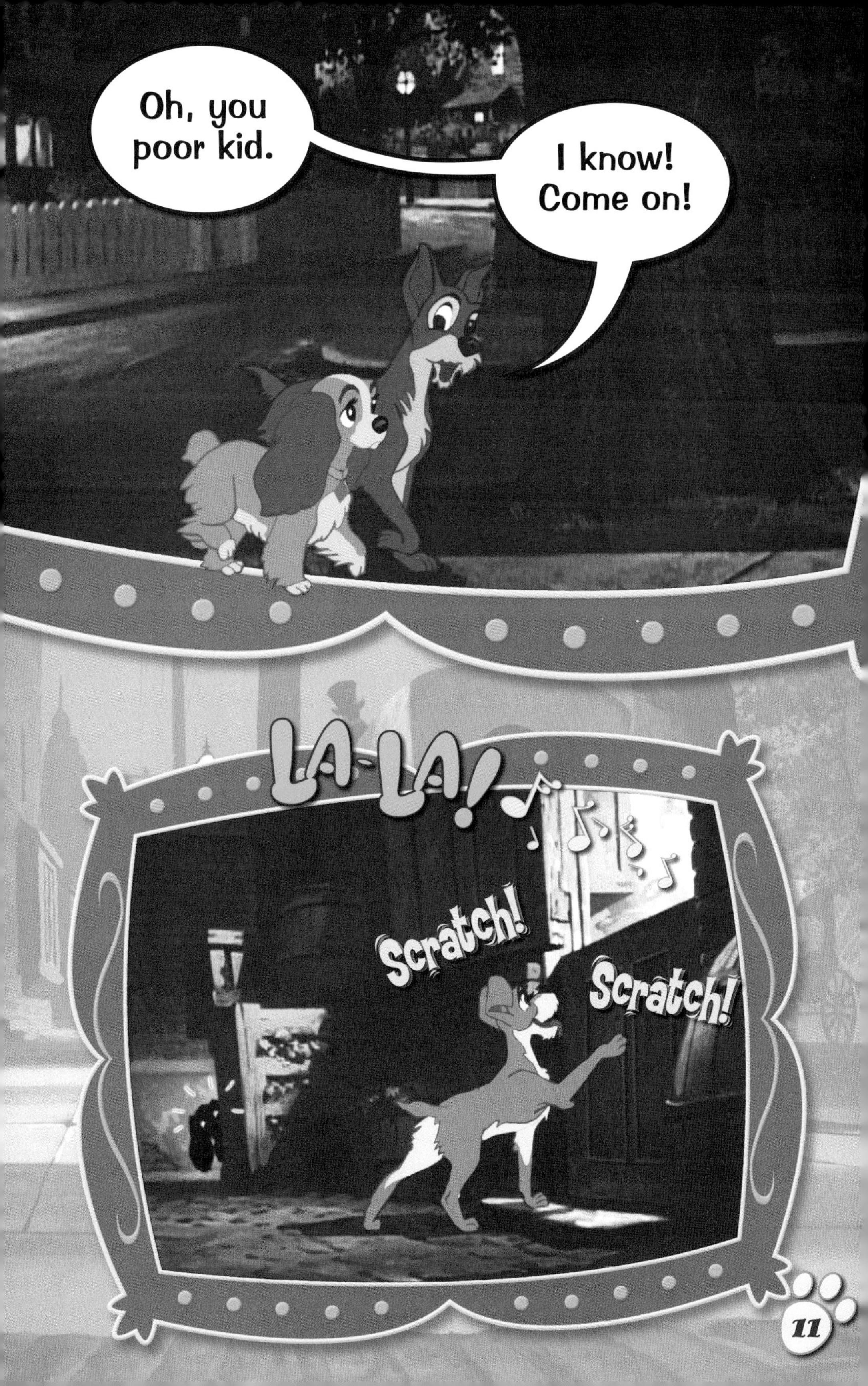
Oh, you poor kid.
I know! Come on!
LA-LA!
Scratch!
Scratch!

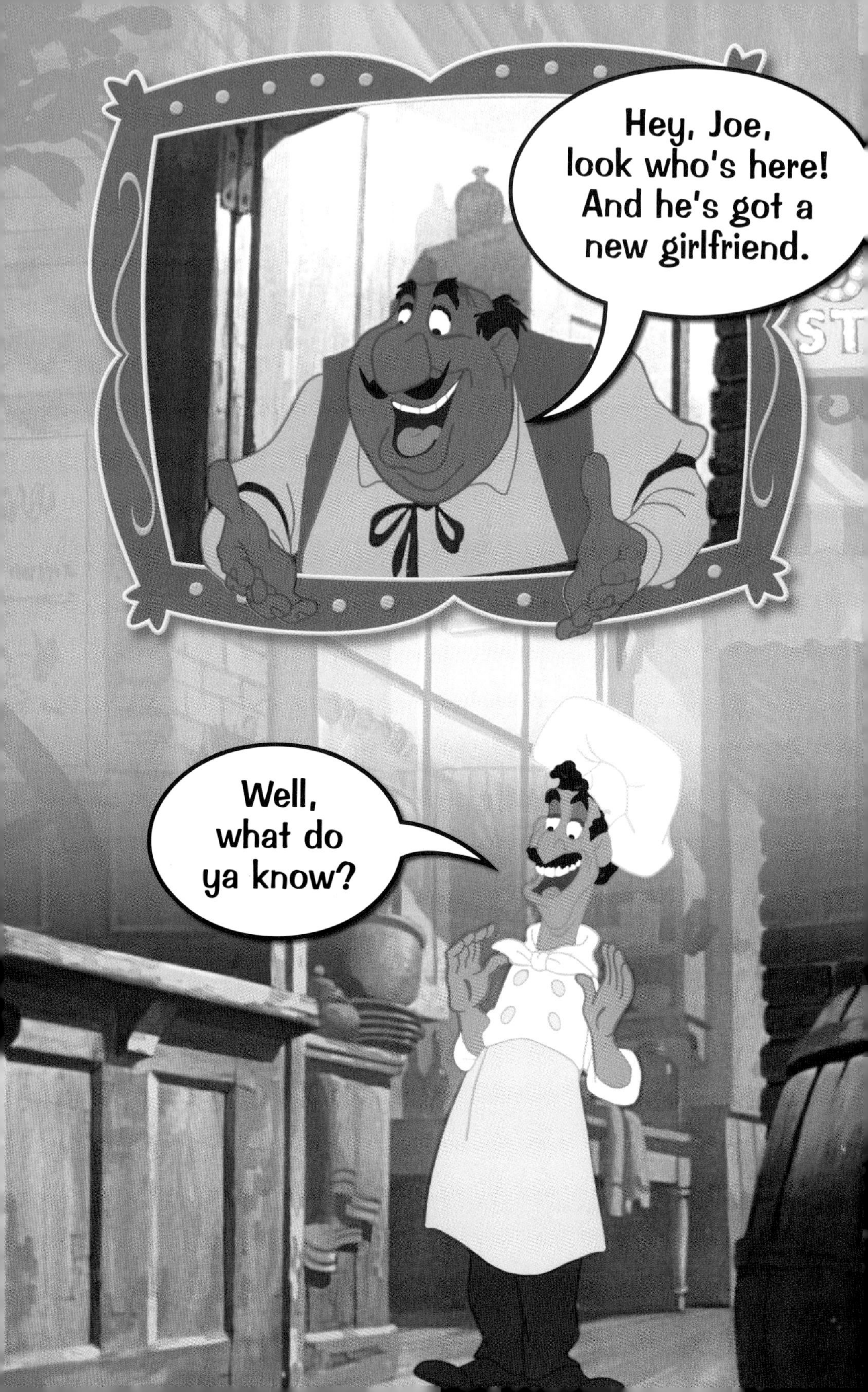
Hey, Joe,
look who's here!
And he's got a
new girlfriend.
Well,
what do
ya know?

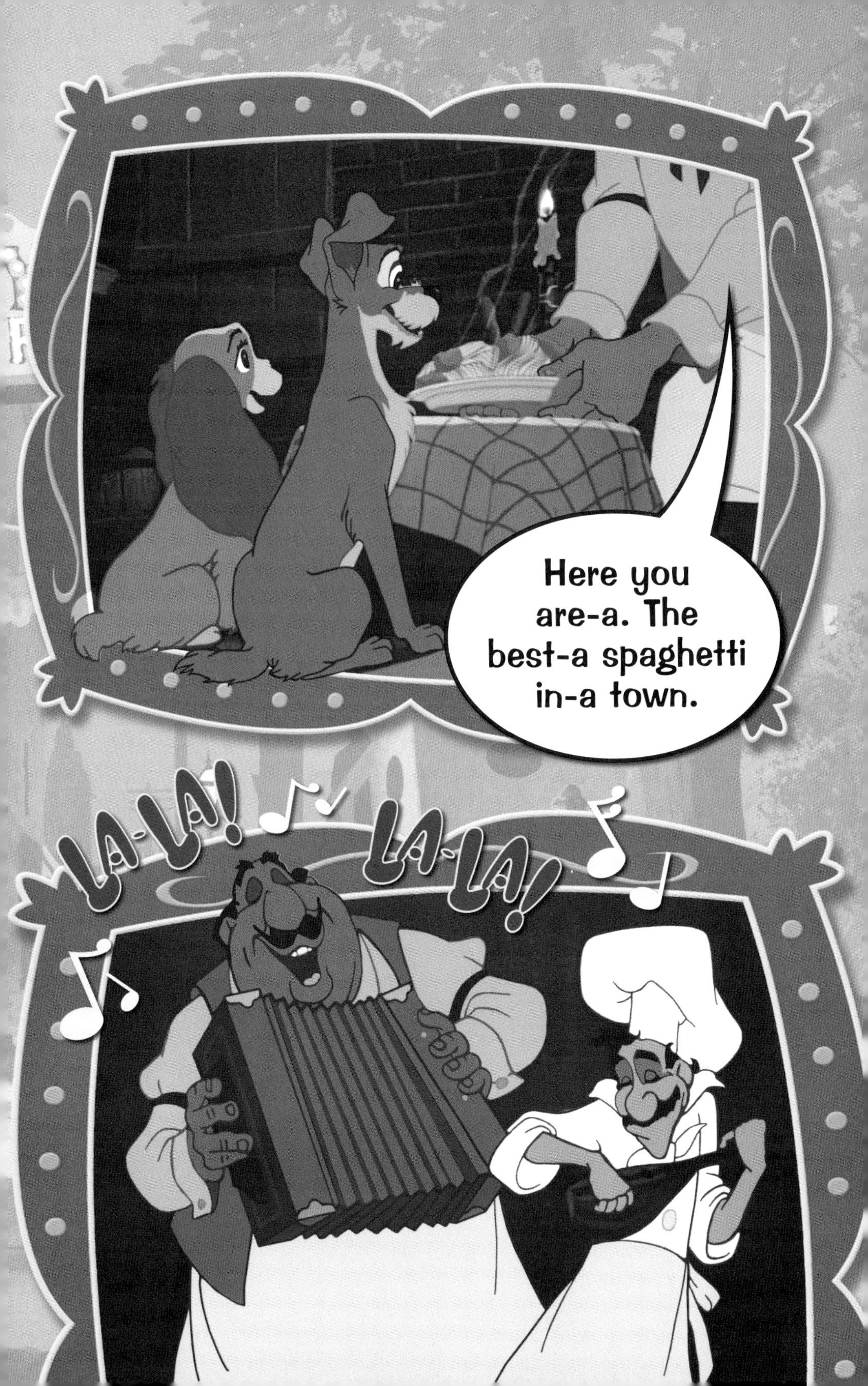
Here you are-a. The best-a spaghetti in-a town.
LA-LA! LA-LA!

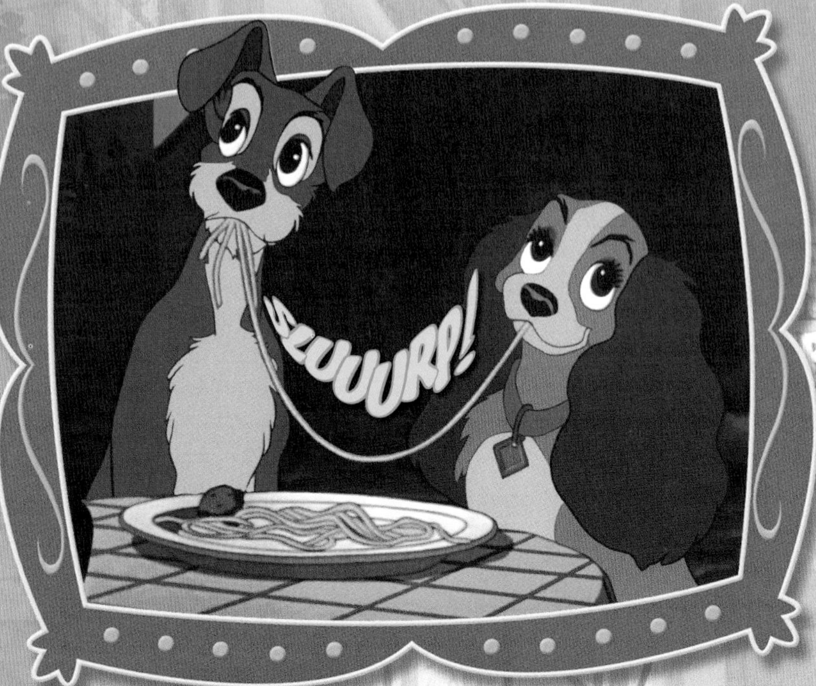
SLUUUURP!

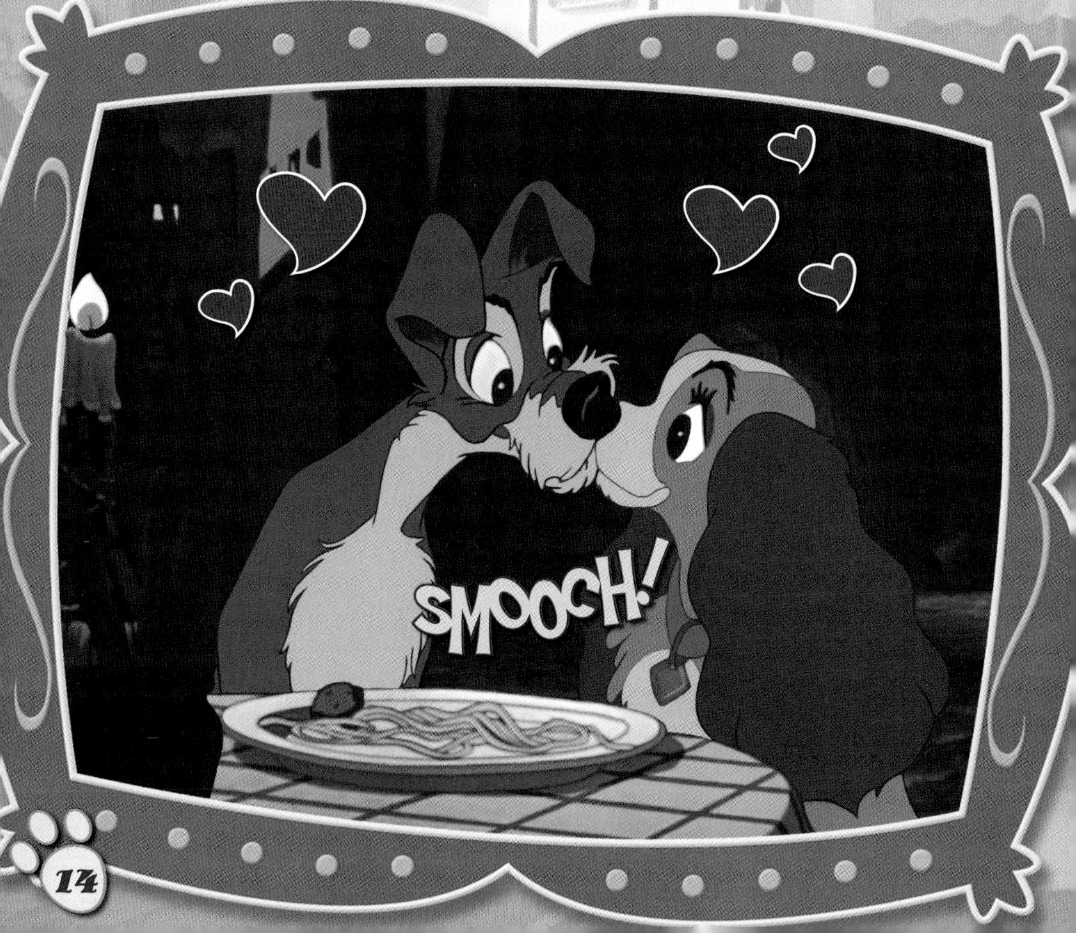
SMOOCH!

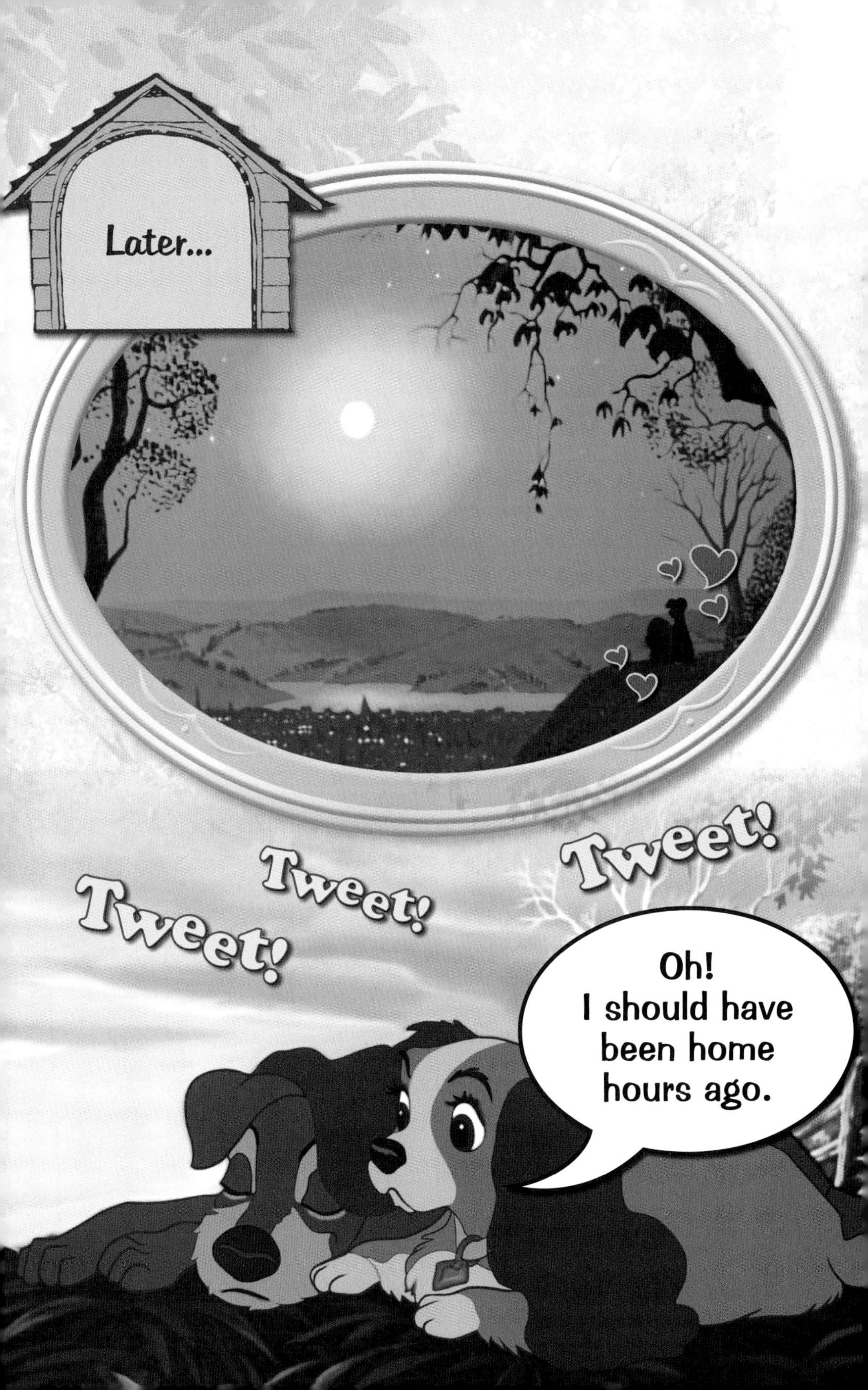
Later...
Tweet!
Tweet!
Tweet!
Oh!
I should have
been home
hours ago.

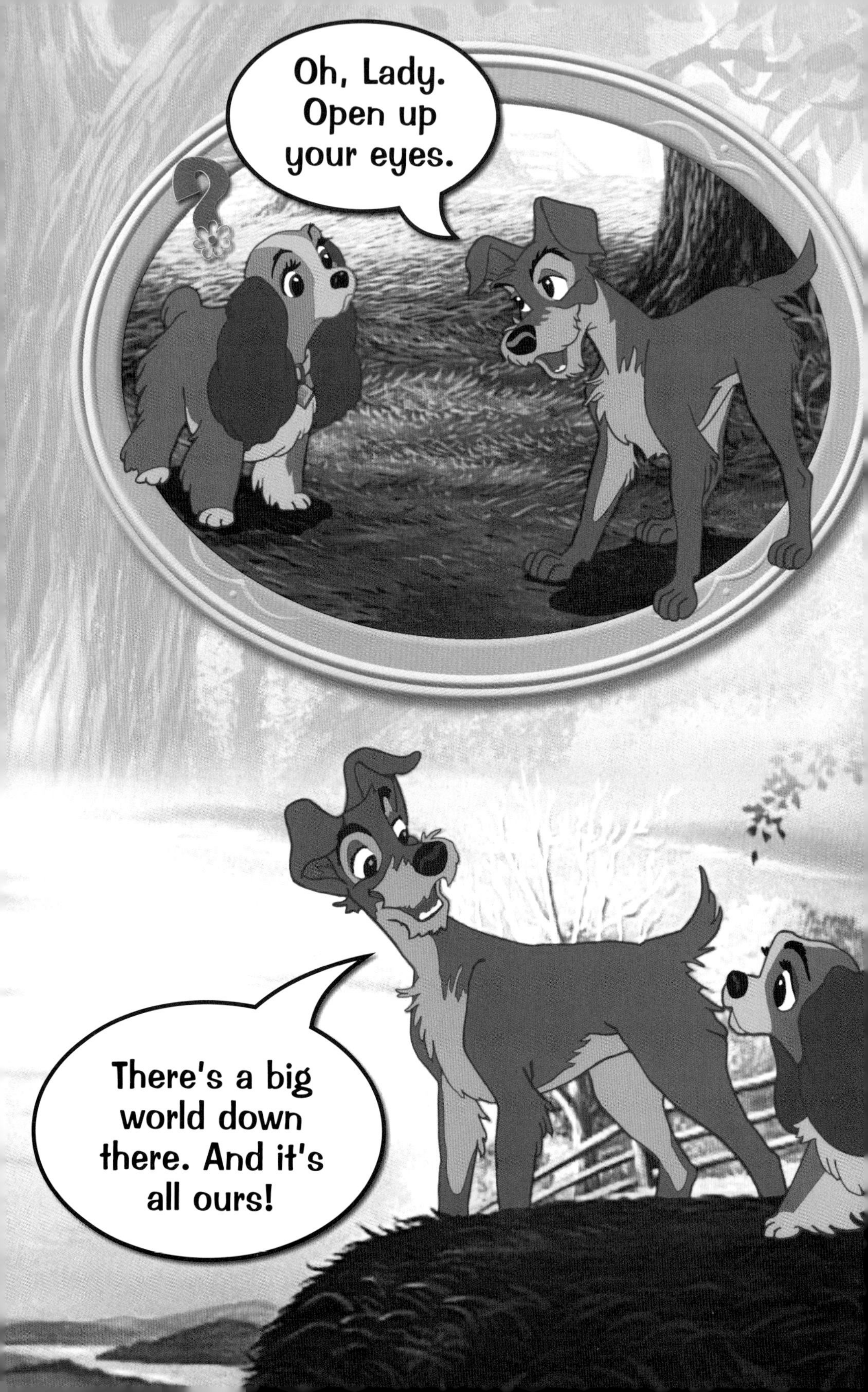
Oh, Lady. Open up your eyes.
There's a big world down there. And it's all ours!

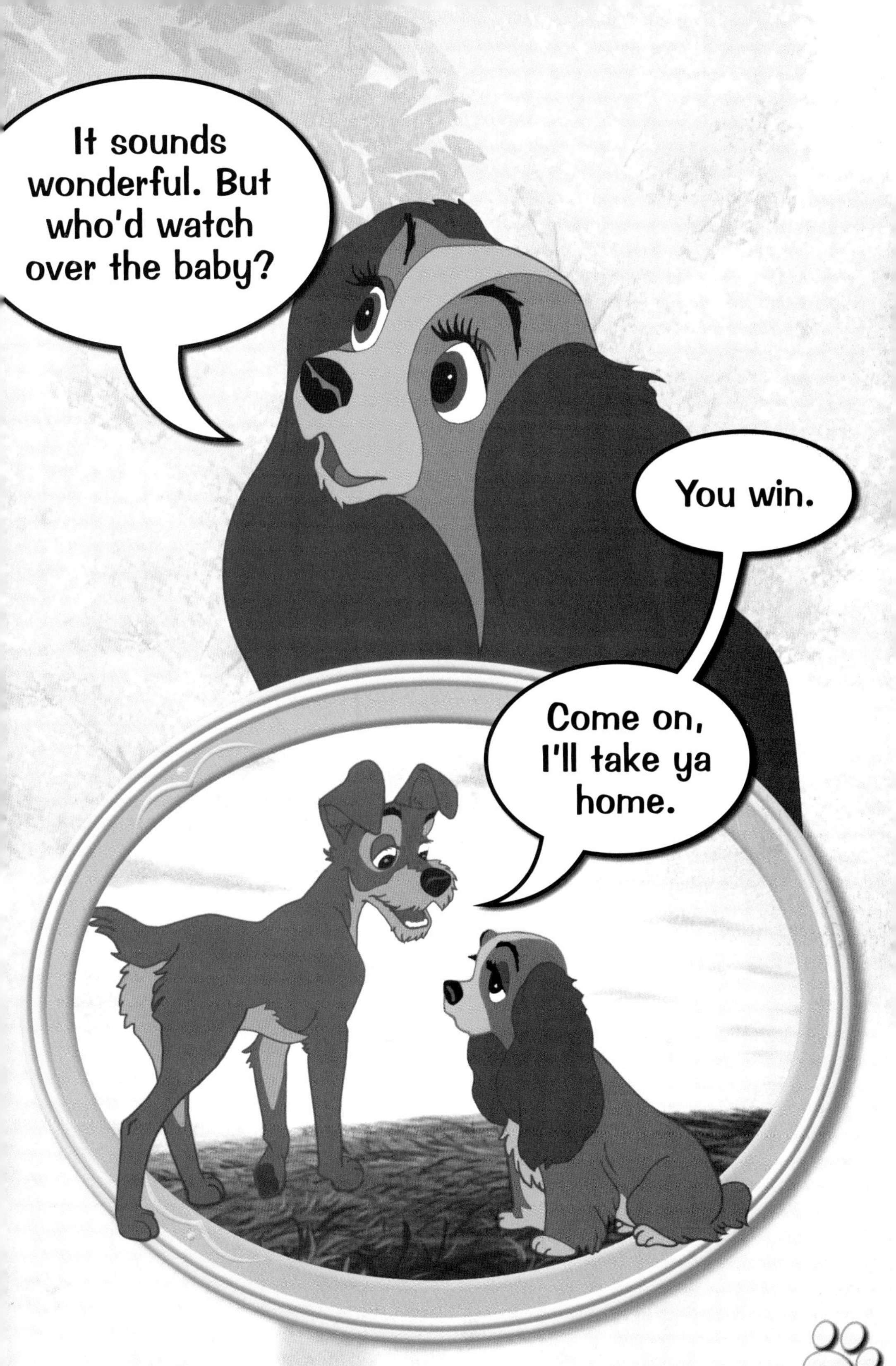
It sounds wonderful. But who'd watch over the baby?
You win.
Come on, I'll take ya home.

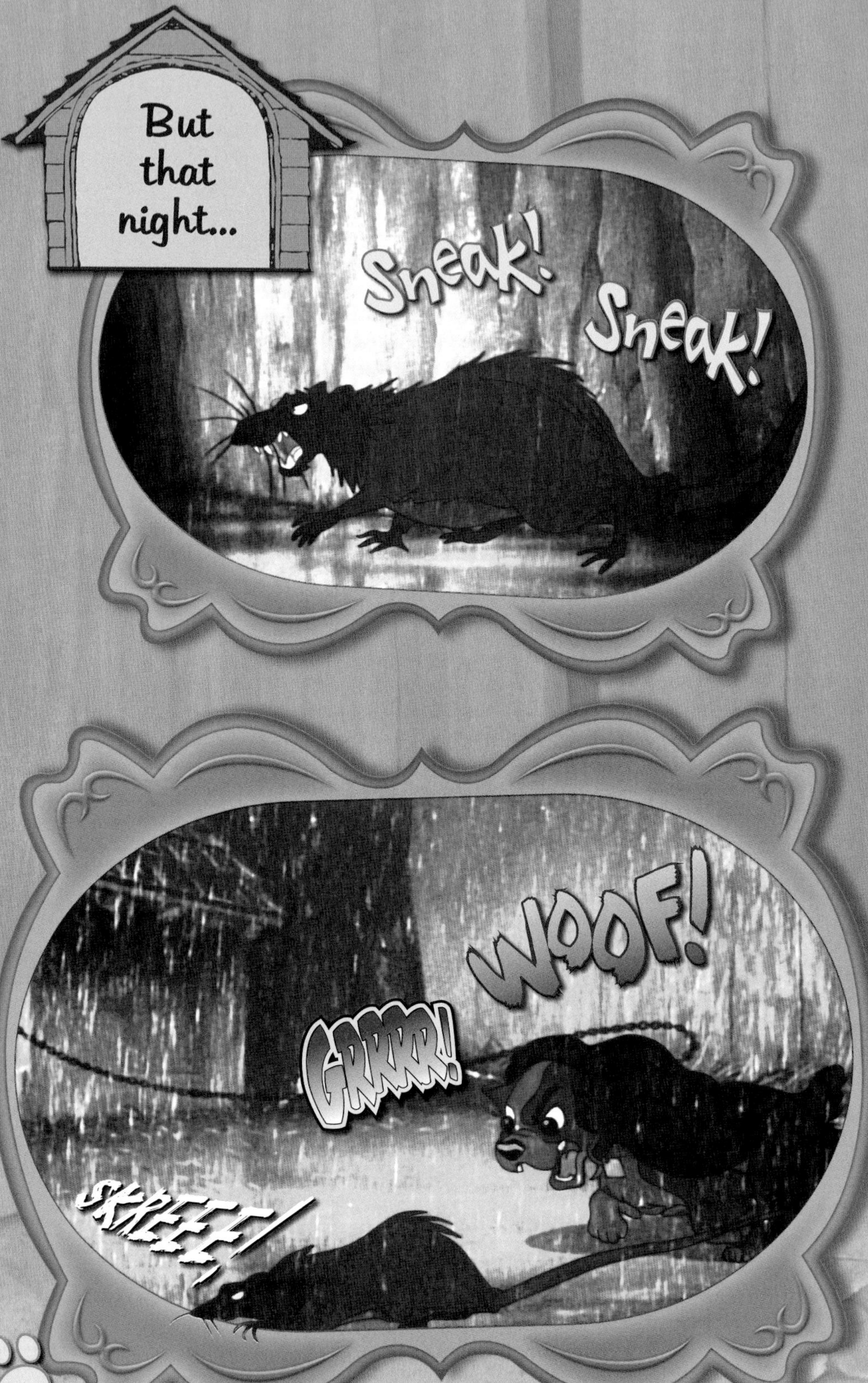
But that night...
Sneak!
Sneak!
WOOF!
GRRRR!
SKREEE!

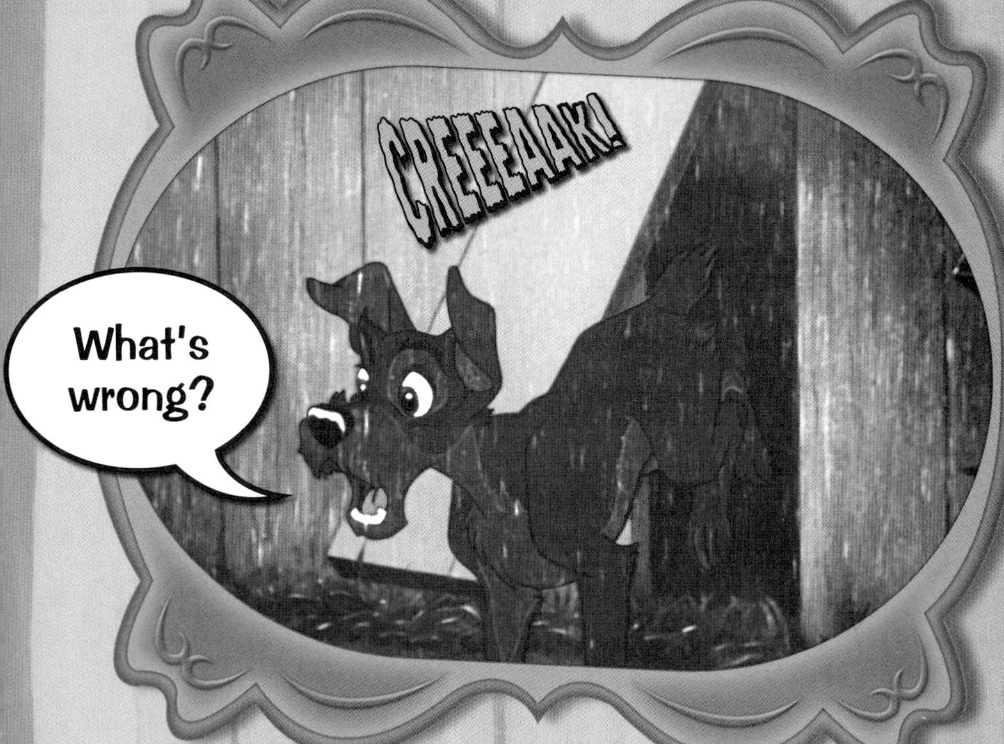
CREEEAAK!
What's wrong?

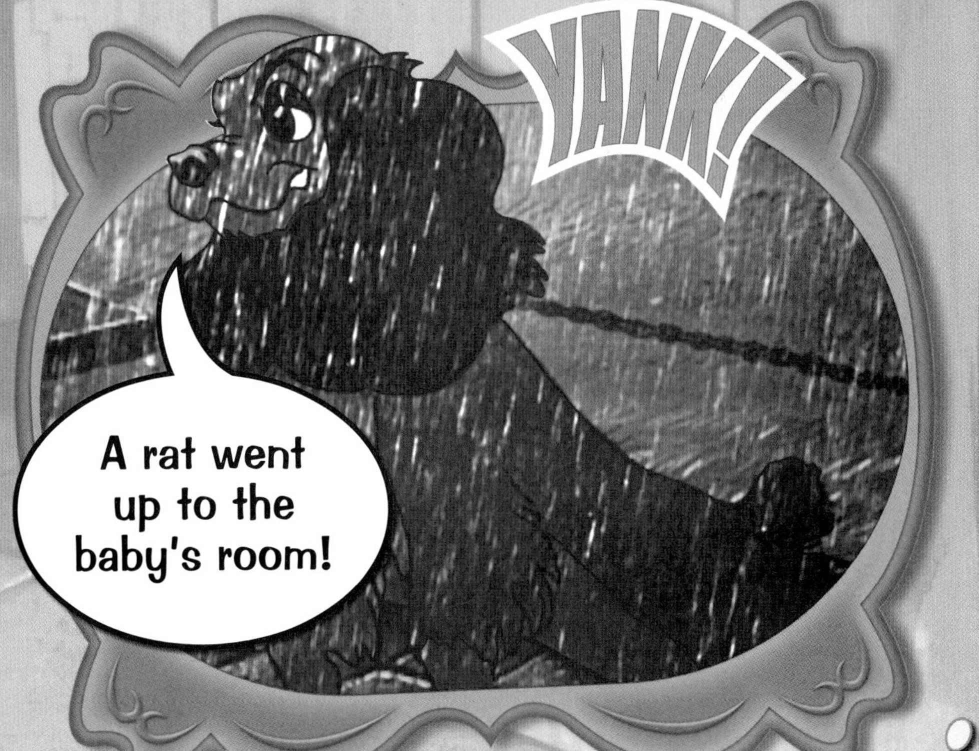
YANK!
A rat went up to the baby's room!

Tramp fought with the rat.

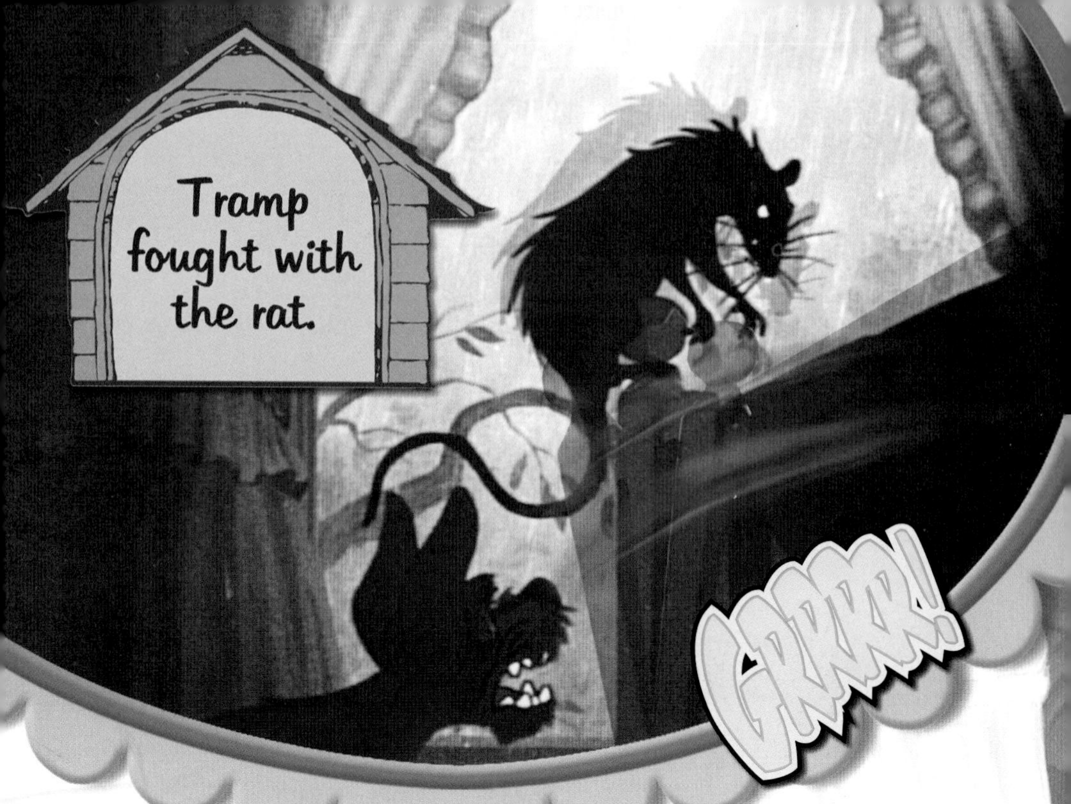
GRRRR!

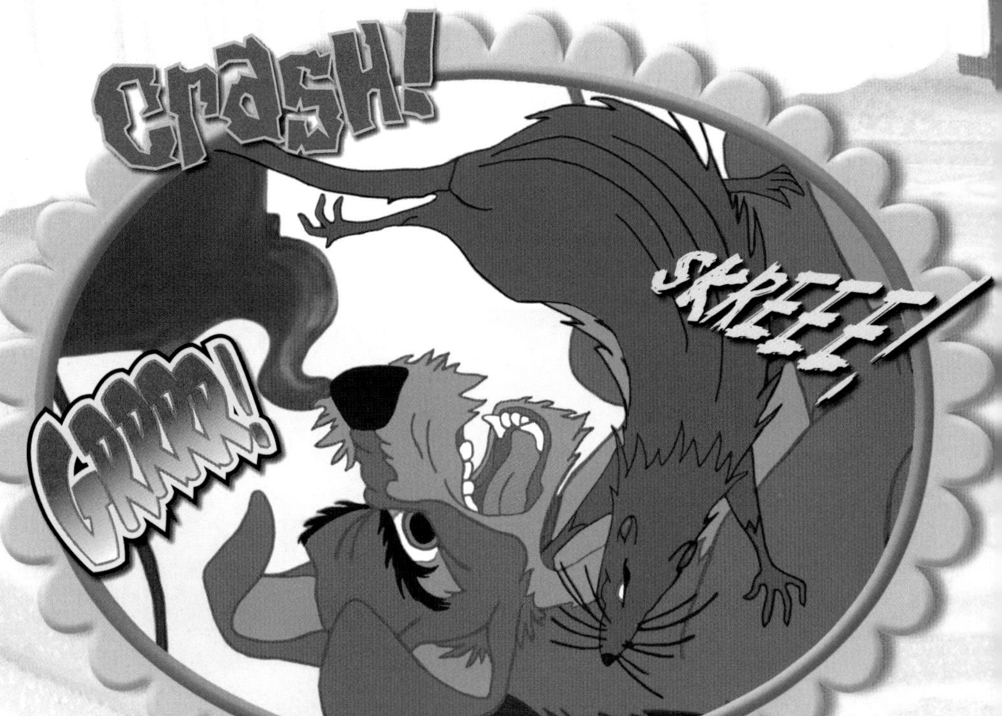
CRASH!
SKREEE!
GRRRR!

Lady broke free and checked on the baby.

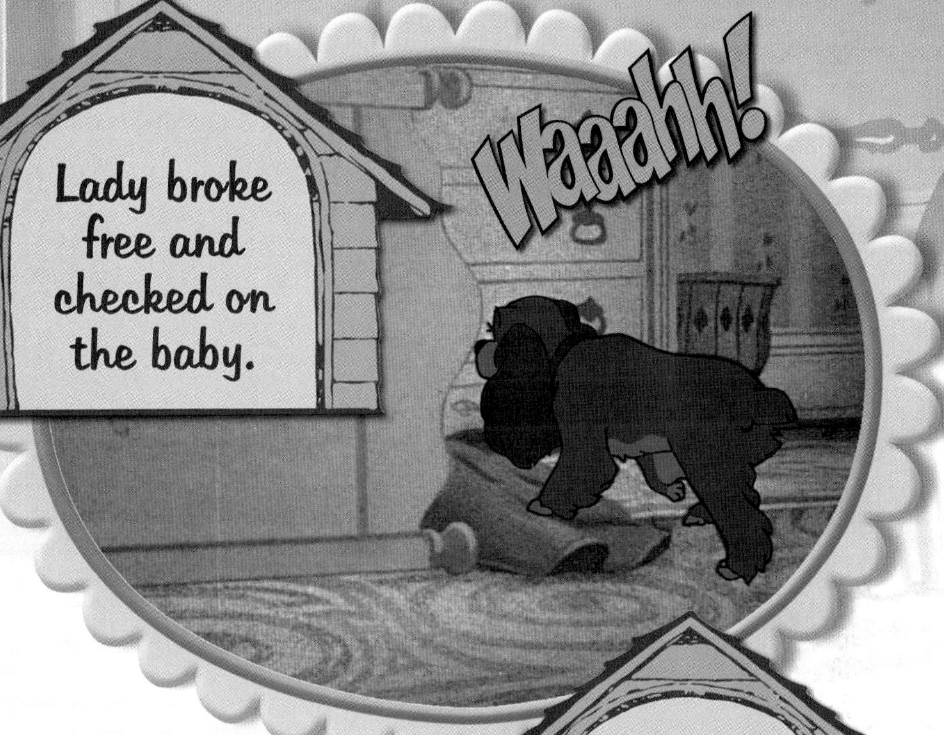
Waaahh!

Tramp took care of the rat.

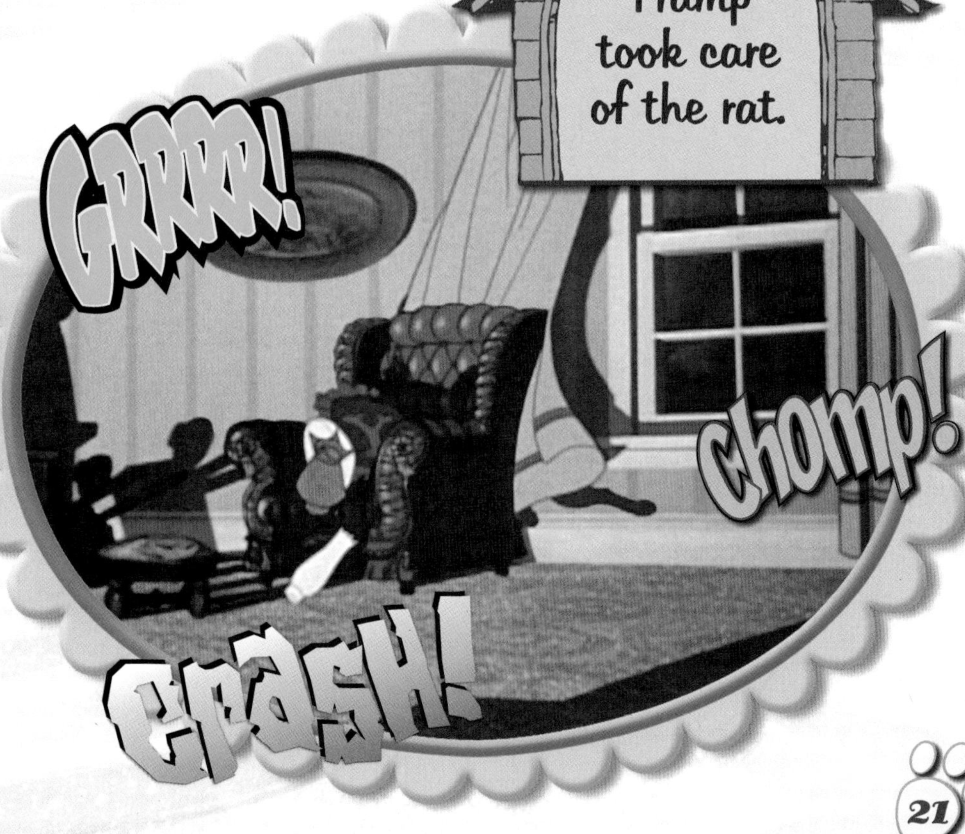
GRRRR!
Chomp!
CRASH!

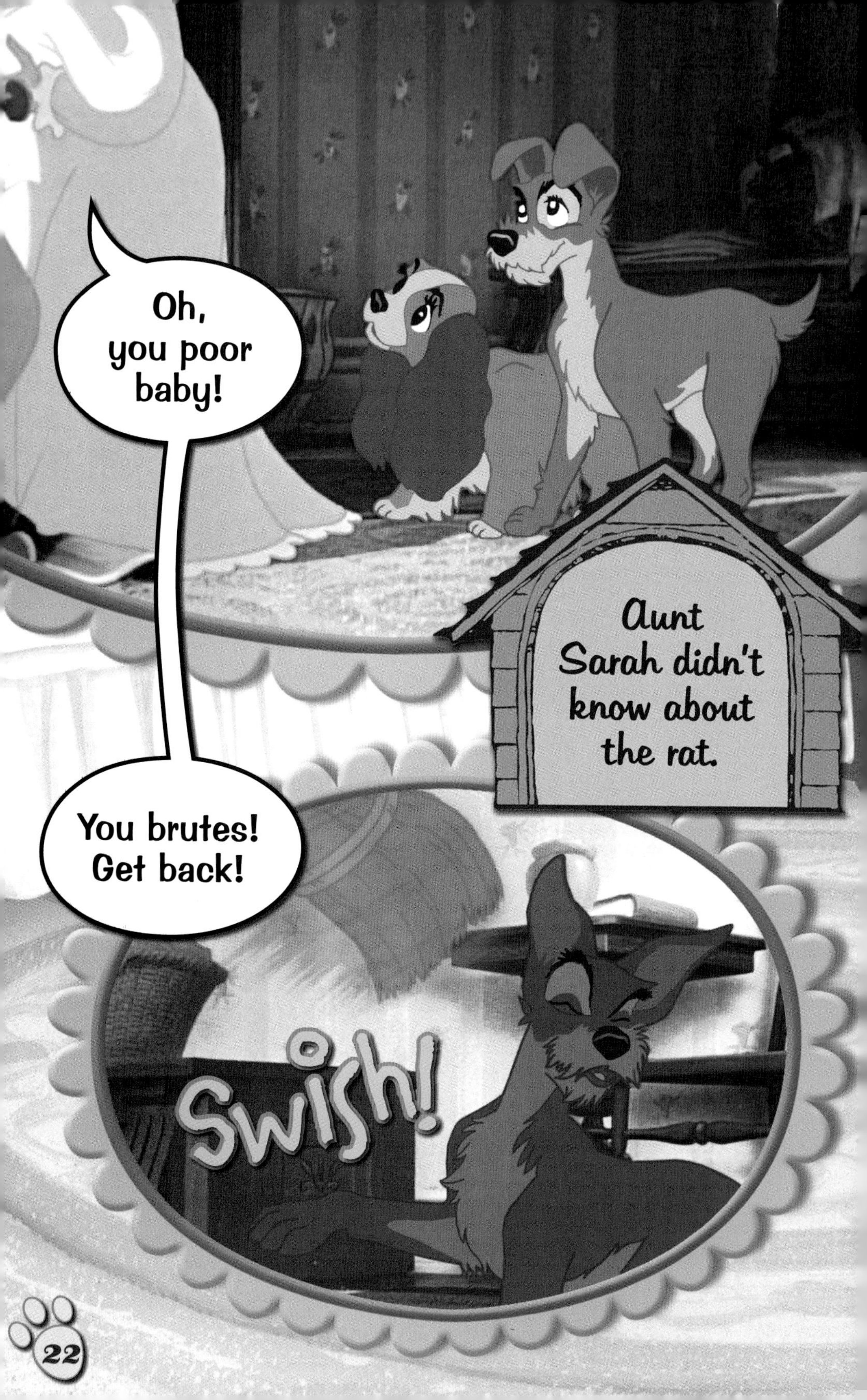

Oh, you poor baby!
Aunt Sarah didn't know about the rat.
You brutes! Get back!
Swish!

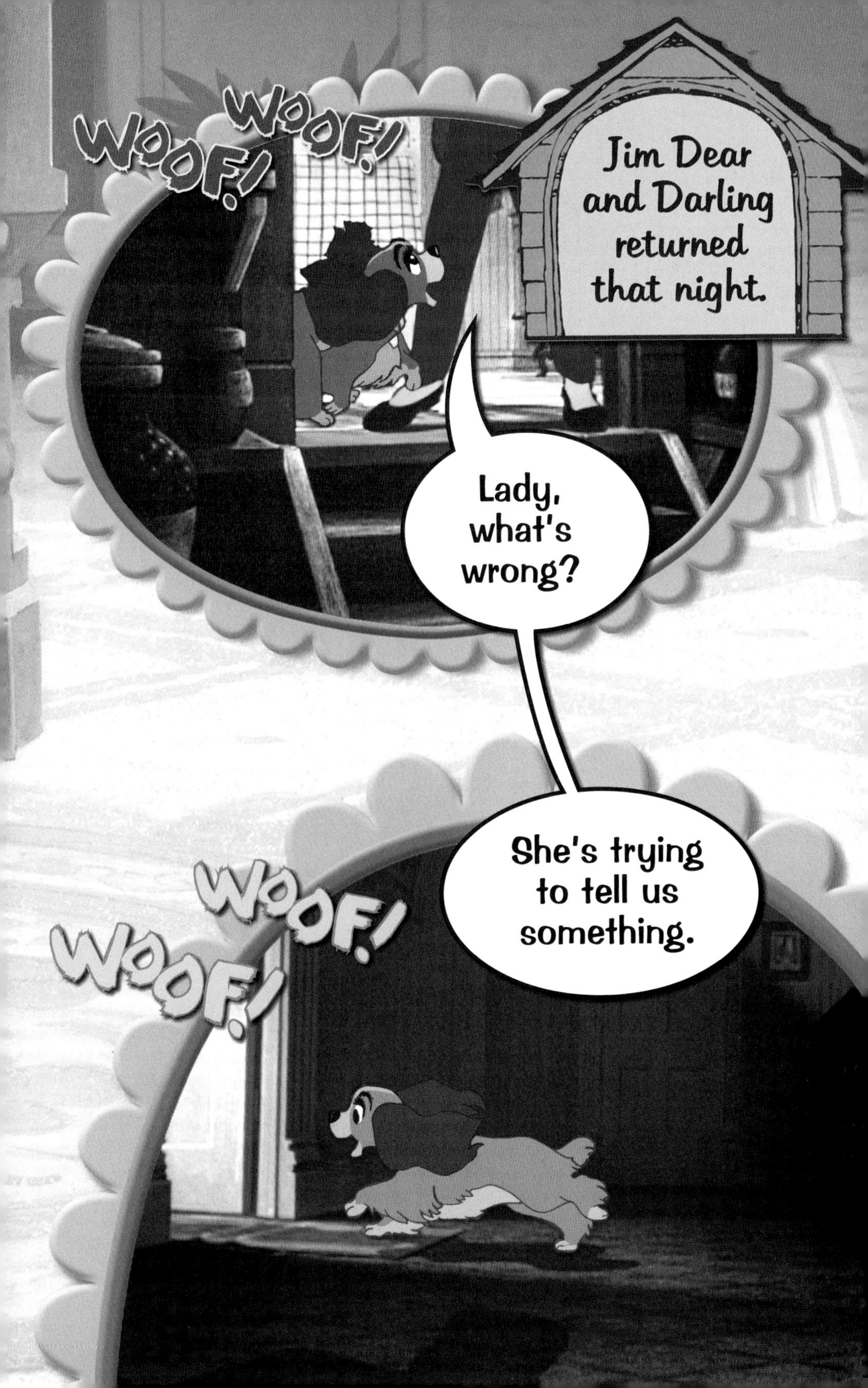
Jim Dear and Darling returned that night.
WOOF! WOOF!
Lady, what's wrong?
She's trying to tell us something.
WOOF! WOOF!

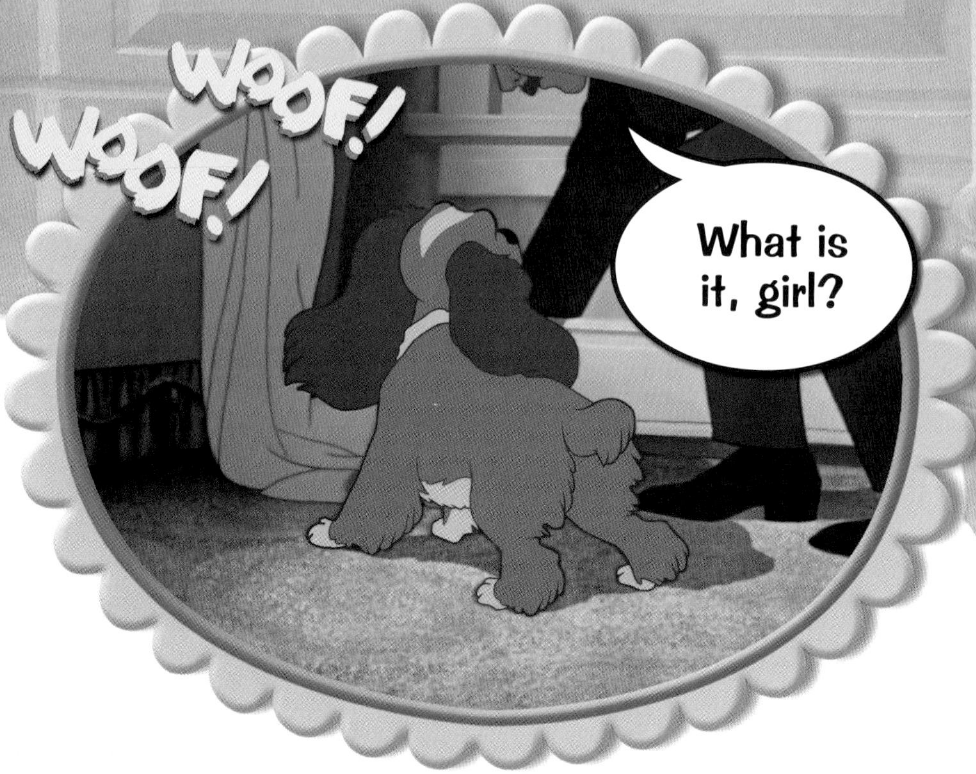
WOOF!
WOOF!
What is it, girl?

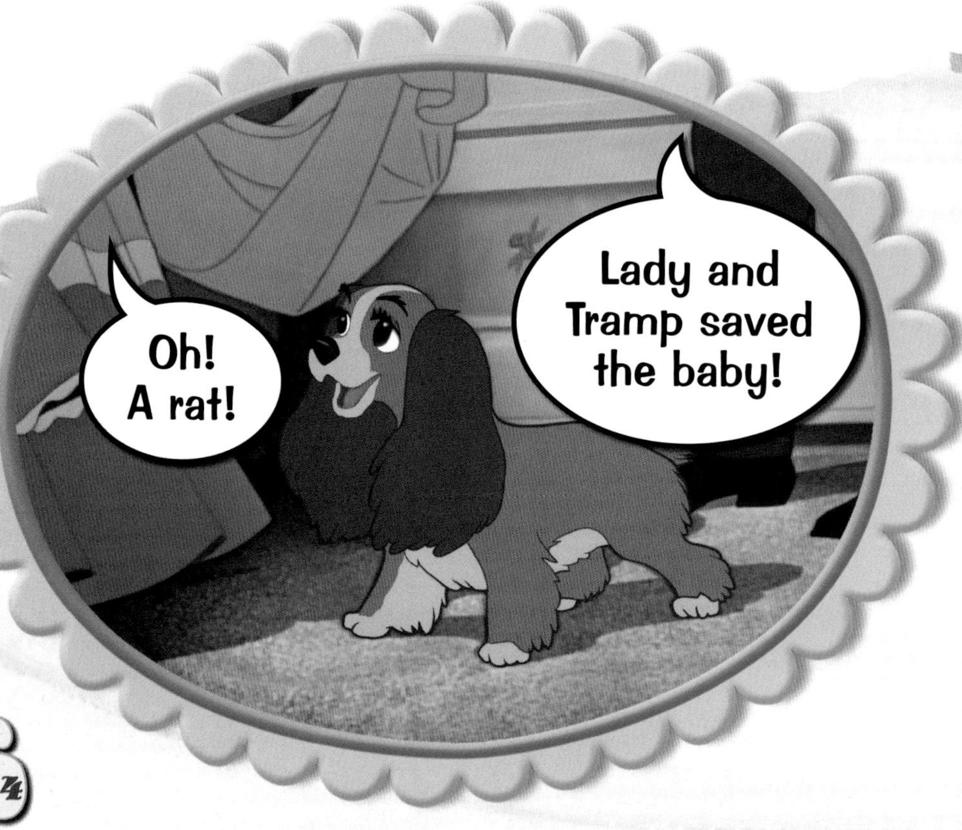
Oh! A rat!
Lady and Tramp saved the baby!

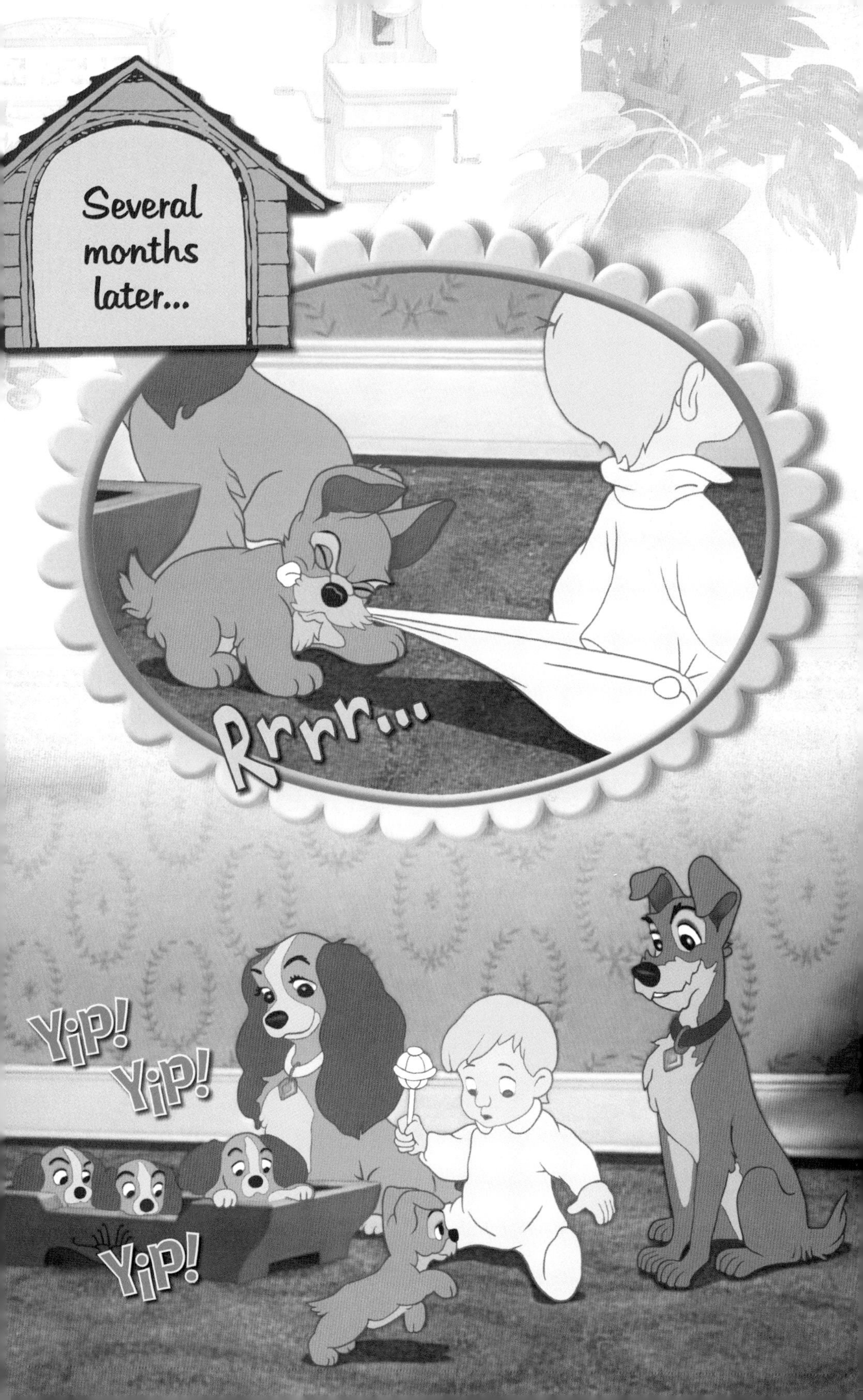

Several months later...
Rrrr...
YIP!
YIP!
YIP!

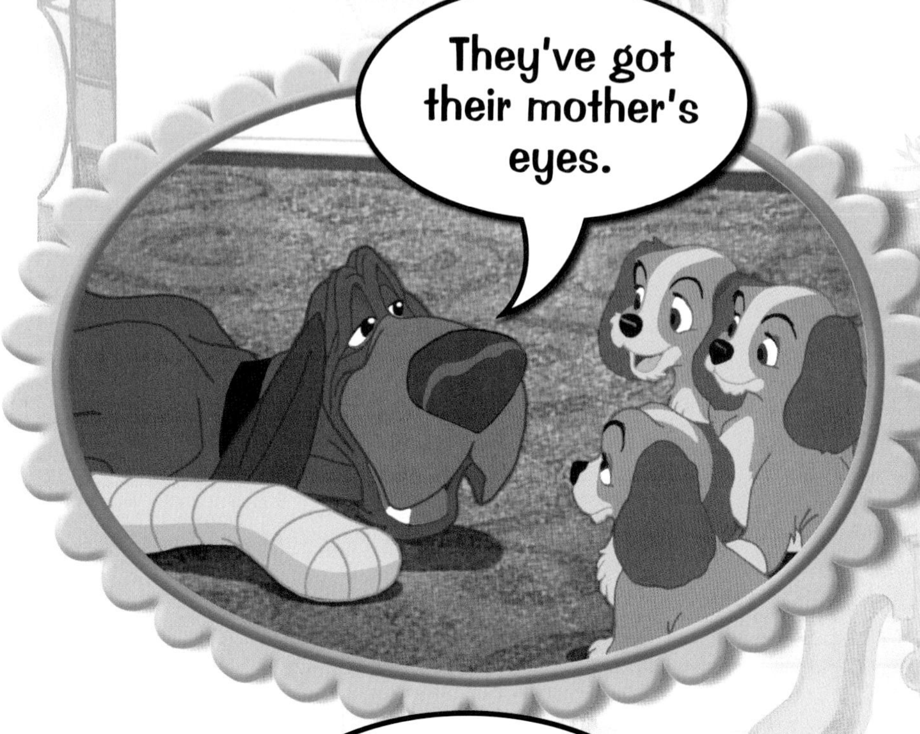
They've got their mother's eyes.

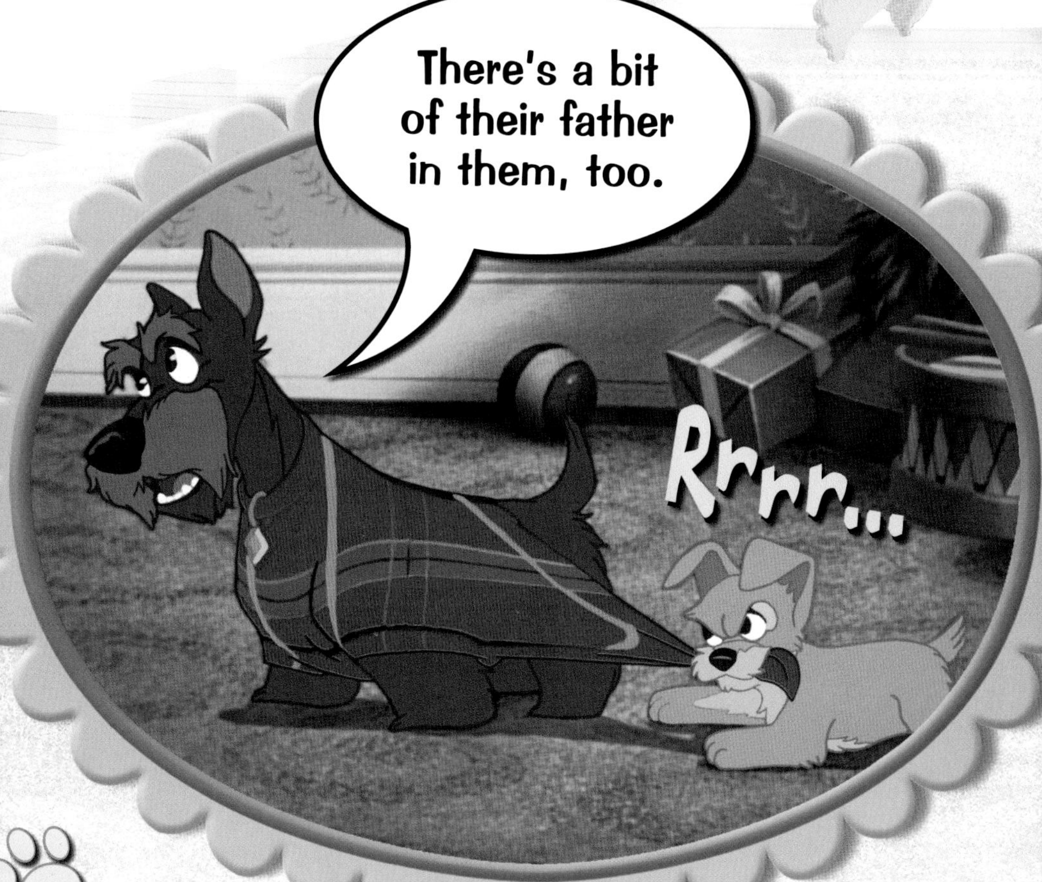
There's a bit of their father in them, too.
Rrrr...

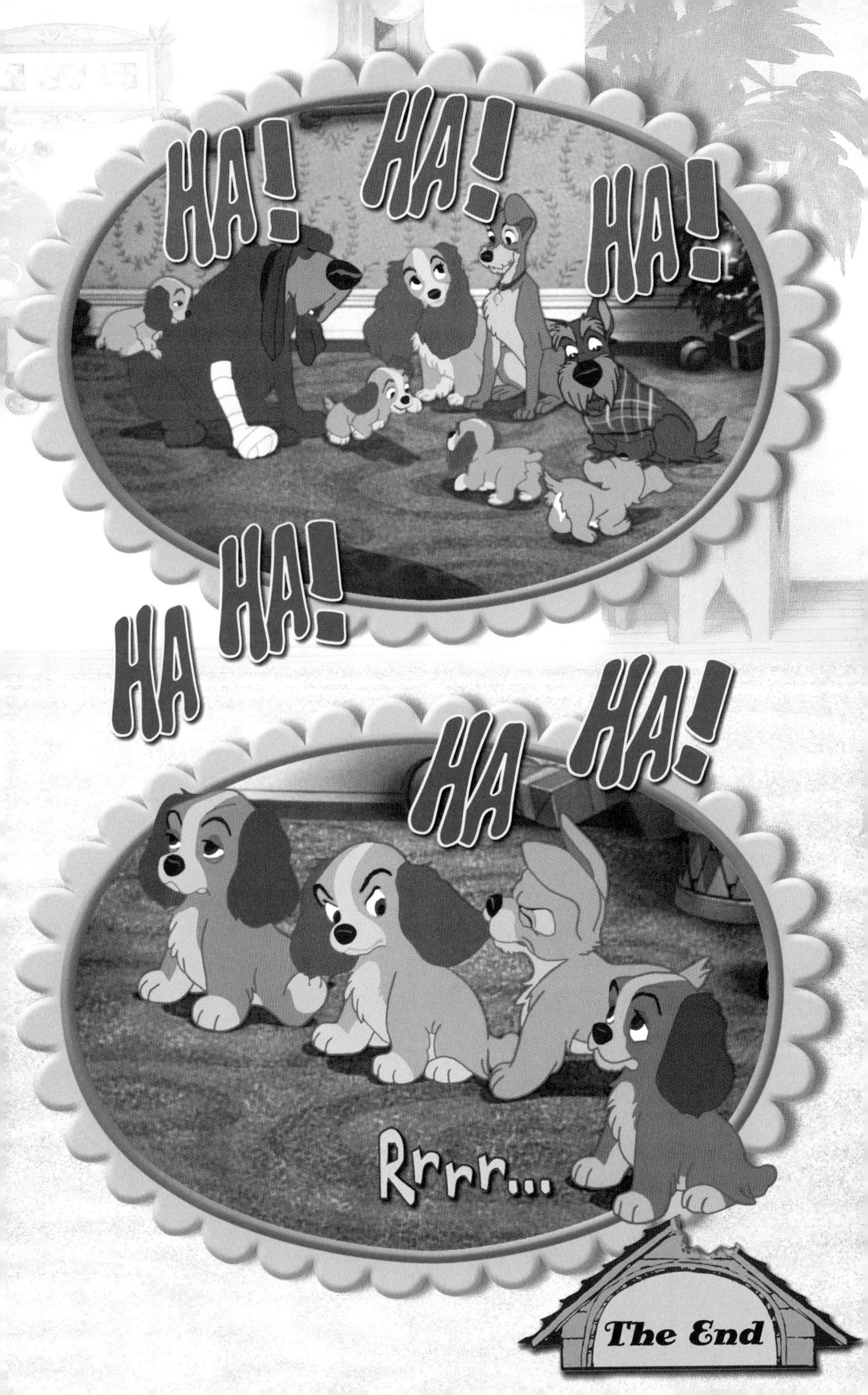
HA! HA! HA!
HA HA!
HA HA!
Rrrr...
The End

CINE-MANGA®

from TOKYOPOP®

Available wherever books are sold.

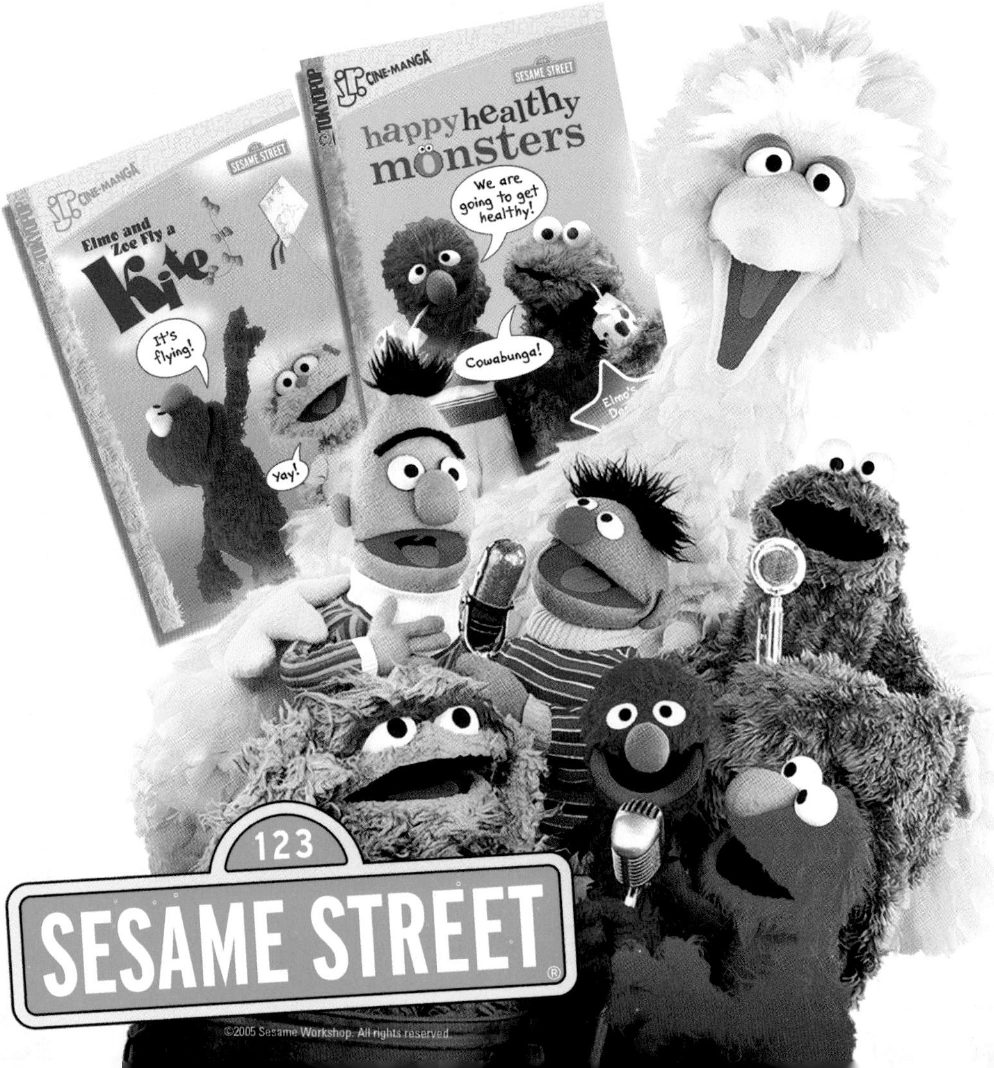
CINE-MANGA
SESAME STREET
TOKYOPOP
Elmo and Zoe Fly a Kite
It's flying!
Yay!
CINE-MANGA
SESAME STREET
TOKYOPOP
happy healthy mönsters
We are going to get healthy!
Cowabunga!
123
SESAME STREET®

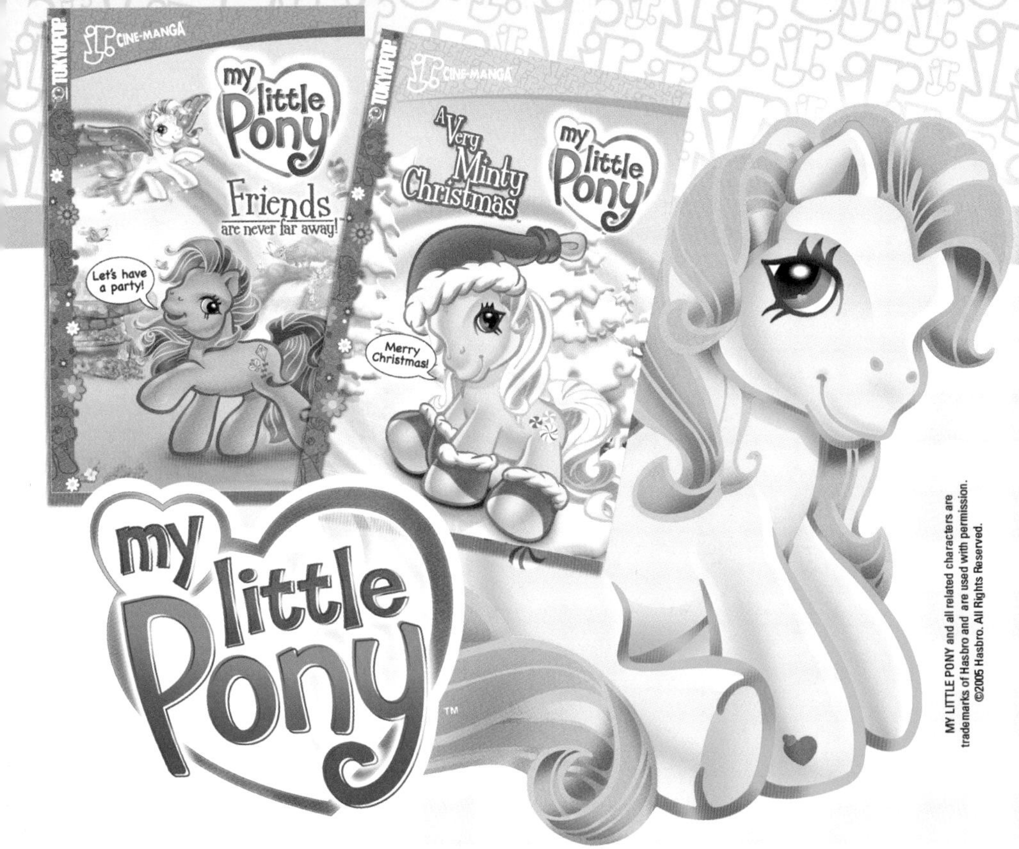
TOKYOPOP
CINE-MANGA
my little Pony
Friends are never far away!
Let's have a party!
TOKYOPOP
CINE-MANGA
A Very Minty Christmas
my little Pony
Merry Christmas!
my little Pony™

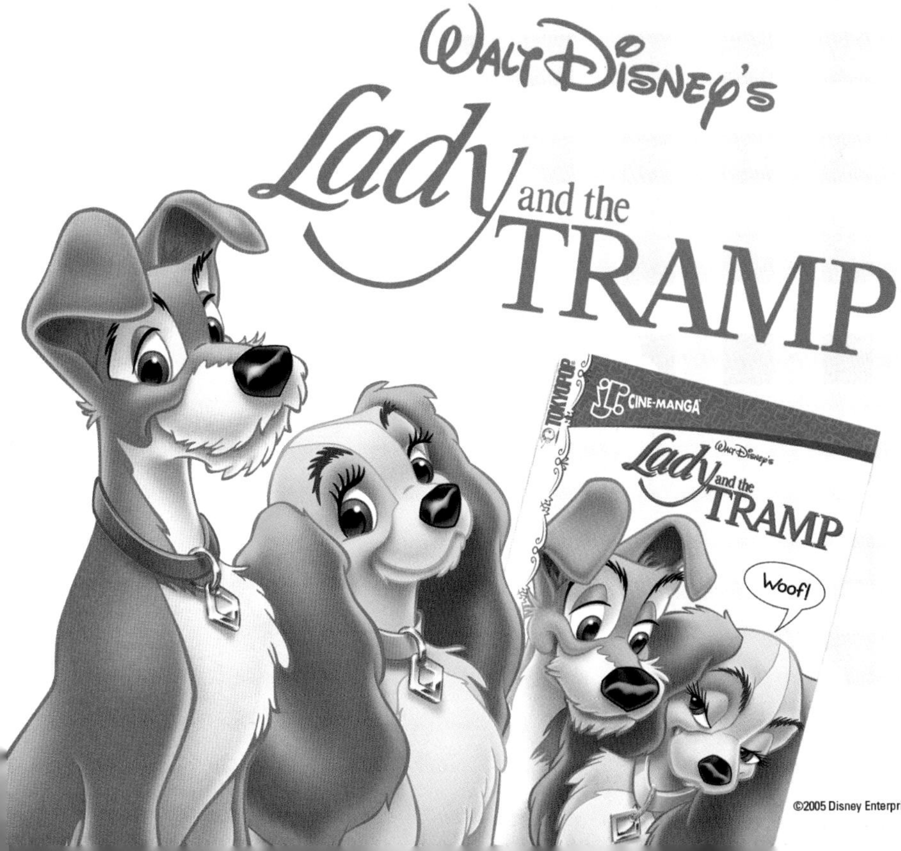
Walt Disney's
Lady and the TRAMP
TOKYOPOP
CINE-MANGA
Walt Disney's
Lady and the TRAMP
Woof!

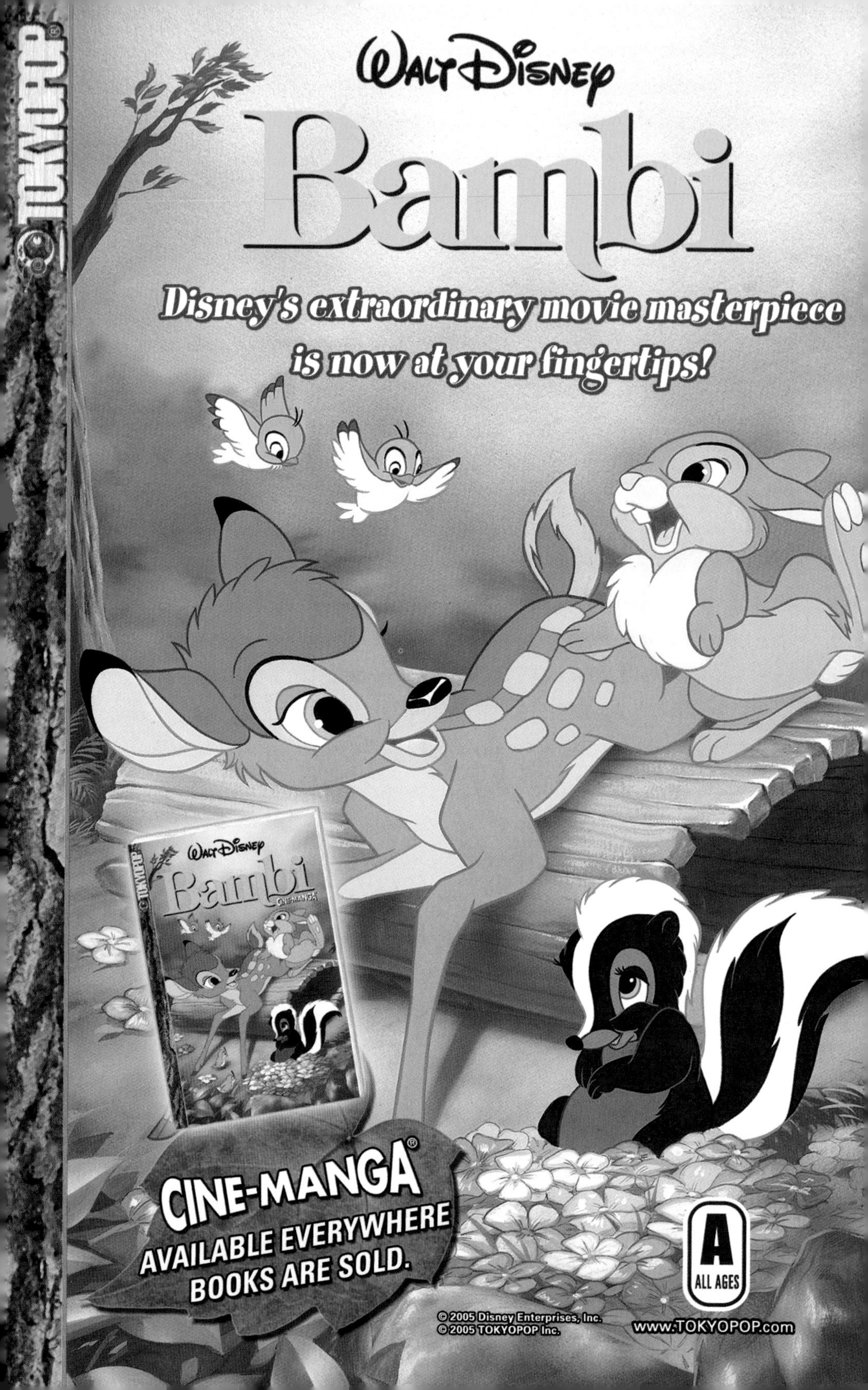

Walt Disney
Bambi
Disney's extraordinary movie masterpiece is now at your fingertips!
CINE-MANGA®
AVAILABLE EVERYWHERE BOOKS ARE SOLD.
A ALL AGES
© 2005 Disney Enterprises, Inc.
© 2005 TOKYOPOP Inc.
www.TOKYOPOP.com

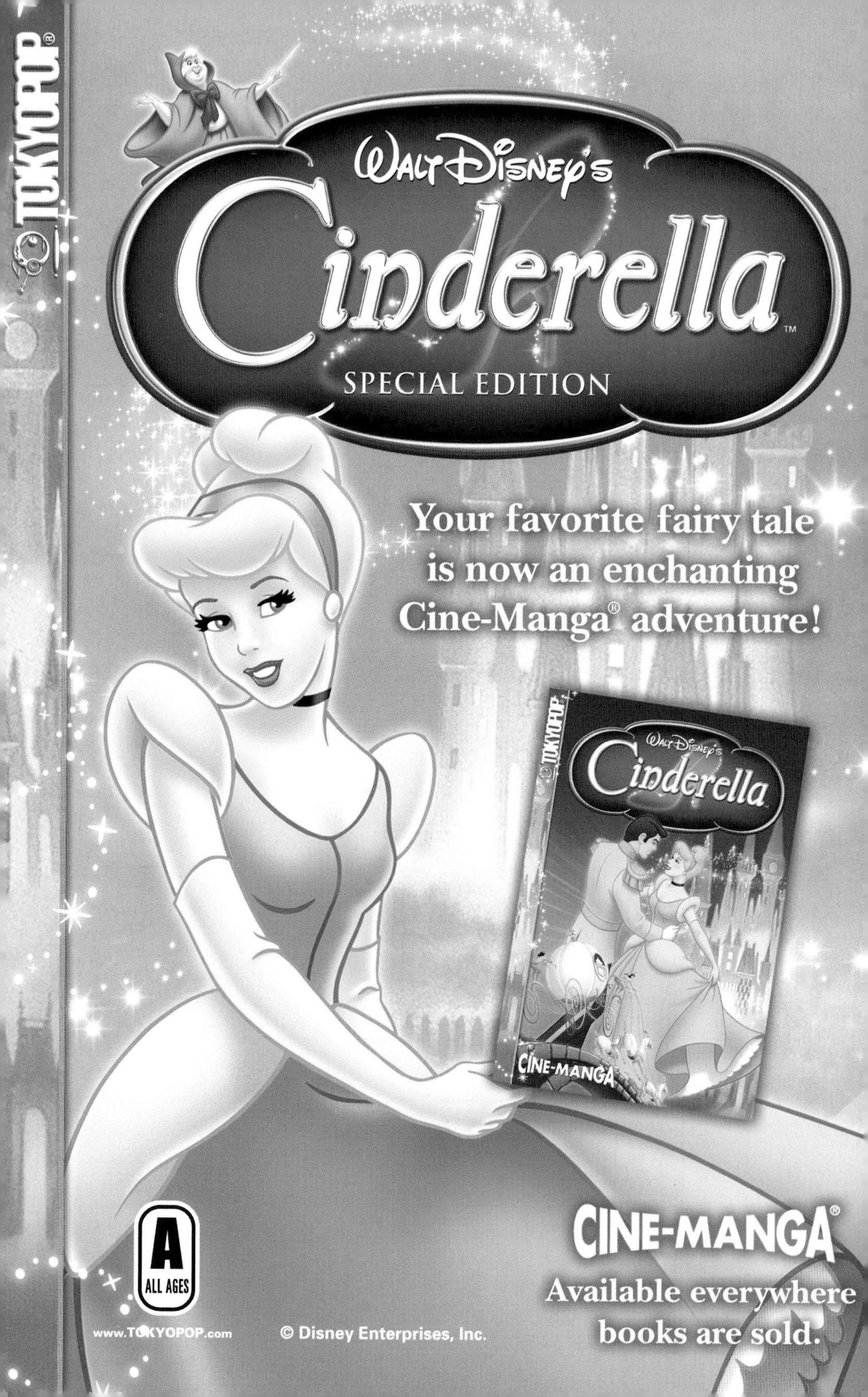

TOKYOPOP
Walt Disney's
Cinderella™
SPECIAL EDITION
Your favorite fairy tale
is now an enchanting
Cine-Manga® adventure!
Walt Disney's
Cinderella
TOKYOPOP
CINE-MANGA
A
ALL AGES
CINE-MANGA®
Available everywhere
books are sold.
www.TOKYOPOP.com
© Disney Enterprises, Inc.